School readiness through play

School readiness through play

How to prepare your child for school from birth – a practical guide

Martie Pieterse

Published by Metz Press
Unit 106, Hoheizen Park 1, Hoheizen Avenue,
Hoheizen 7530

First edition 2001

Editor	Wilsia Metz
Translator	Ethné Clarke
Cover design	Metz Press
Designer	jack, Boston
Illustrations	Anette van Zyl
Production coordinator	Andrew de Kock
Reproduction	CIB, Cape Town
Printing and binding	Creda Communication, Epping
ISBN	1-875001-20-4

Contents

Foreword

This book fulfils a need that has existed among parents for many years. Martie Pieterse has combined her more than 30 years of experience in pre-primary teaching and her theoretical knowledge to put together an extremely useful manual, which enables parents to stimulate all the facets of their child's development. The information is easy to understand and is applicable to parents from all communities in society. The developmental phases of children from newborn to six years give parents a clear yardstick for measuring the development of their own children.

Martie gives examples of everyday things in and around the house to be used for games and activities. Consequently, stimulation is not only pleasurable, but also affordable.

Prevention is always better than treatment. Backlogs [?handicaps sounds too alarming?] in development are often only identified when children are already in their pre-primary year or at school, or sometimes not identified at all. By the time it is realised that there is a problem, these children are often showing secondary emotional problems, such as lack of self-confidence or behavioural problems, to mention only a few. These children then need professional help, which is not only time consuming, but also fairly expensive.

Kahlil Gibran said: 'You are the bows from which your children as living arrows are set forth. ... Let your bending in the archer's hand be for gladness.'

I have enjoyed the privelege of working with Martie for some years, and have seen her in action. Children blossomed under her guidance.

Rose Prins
Occupational therapist

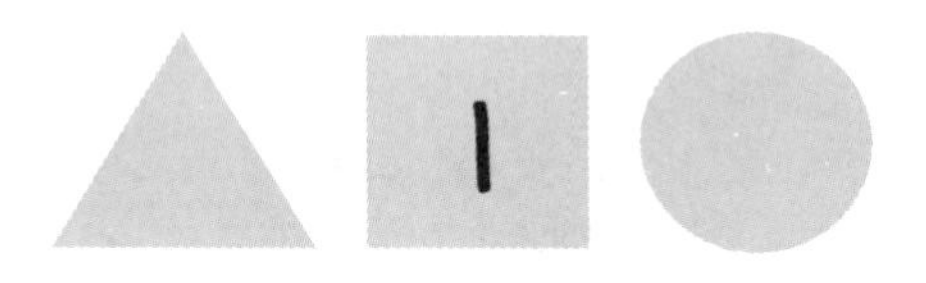

Introduction: play and learn

It is generally accepted that children's genes determine their maximum development potential, while the environment in which they grow up determines how much of this potential they will realise.

When to start

Children begin learning at birth – in fact, even before they are born. Research has shown that activity in the brain of a foetus can be observed as early as eight to twelve weeks after conception. The nerve cells that carry electrical impulses through the nervous system to the brain are not aimless impulses; they have a specific purpose in the development of the brain. These impulses received by the brain cells change the physical shape of the brain as the foetus develops, and form connecting patterns or channels which the brain will use to function.

Develop the potential

With a few exceptions, every baby is born with boundless brain potential that must be developed. The only way this potential can be developed, is by stimulation. A new-born baby is ready to get to know his new world. That is why your task of making your child ready for school and learning begins the moment he opens his eyes.

From the very beginning, he wants to make the acquaintance of the people and things around him. He is poised for learning – the most receptive and eager pupil you could ever have. You have to provide the stimulation for this learning process, and the best possible learning environment to enable him to reach his full potential.

The first five to six years of a child's life are the most important years for the development of language, learning skills, a positive self-image, self-confidence, concentration and perseverance – the cornerstones of school-readiness. This is when the foundations are laid for everything that follows. There is no other time in a child's life when he learns as much as in the first five years.

How children learn

Initially, children learn by trial and error, and by imitation. They can be taught more formally at a later stage. But in the exciting period before they begin school, children learn through play.

You can transform every interaction with your child into a game, and each game will become an opportunity for learning. Make time to play with your child and you will be giving both yourself and your child a precious gift. Through play, you can develop your child's learning skills and language ability, channel his natural enthusiasm, curiosity, thirst for knowledge, and energy, and create opportunities for promoting his self-confidence, social and emotional growth, co-ordination and problem-solving ability. Play offers children an easy way of learning while having fun.

School-maturity and school-readiness

Before your child can go to school, she must be school-mature as well as school-ready. It is important for you to know the diference.

What is school-maturity?

Maturity is a natural process of growth and development that is not influenced by practising or learning specific skills to any great extent. This does not mean that all children mature at the same pace, but only that there are certain milestones that indicate when something is wrong. Within these milestones your child progresses at her own pace. It does not make sense to expect something from your child before she has the necessary physical or mental equipment, or maturity. When she is psychologically ready to undertake certain tasks, and is sufficiently developed physically, she will succeed. For this reason school-maturity cannot be forced – it must be anticipated.

What does school-readiness mean?

School-readiness is a larger concept that includes school-maturity. It implies that your child has reached a stage of development where she can benefit from formal school tutorship with minimum tension. School-readiness can be consciously encouraged by stimulation in all the developmental areas, rich experiences, and creative play. When a child is school-ready, she will be able to meet the demands of the school.

What is expected when a child goes to school?

- Normal, healthy physical development
- Large muscle development (gross motor skills)
- Small muscle development (fine motor skills, such as hand-eye, and foot-eye co-ordination)
- To be able to think, distinguish, and understand
- Perceptual development
- Intellectual development
- Can learn
- Wants to learn
- Concentration and perseverance (attention span)
- Language skills (listening skills)
- To be emotionally and socially well-adjusted (includes moral development, conscience)

Your role as a parent

The demands made on a child who goes to school clearly show that school-readiness involves far more than the necessary intellectual development. Social maturity, emotional stability, self-confidence and physical health are equally important. All these develop against a background of love and acceptance at home – an environment in which your child feels secure enough to discover and learn new things – to take risks and to reach out. All that is required from you is to love your child, and to have a basic knowledge of her development. With knowledge of how your child develops and gains her knowledge of the world, you will be able to ensure that, through your interaction with her, she will start off well – and, with the necessary stimulation, that she will remain on the right track.

Your toddler's first day at school is the beginning of many years on the school benches – the beginning of a period in which many demands will be made on her and a lot of pressure will be put on her. Your contribution to her success at school is invaluable, and your responsibility for her readiness for school at the appropriate time begins at her birth. It is not something that can be put off until the year before she starts school, and it is not a responsibility that can be delegated to a pre-primary school. So, arm yourself with as much knowledge as possible and approach the task with as much energy and enthusiasm as your child shows.

About the book

The chapters in this book are divided according to a child's various areas of development – from sensory perception to her emotional and social development. We will take a look at the importance of play in your child's life, followed by a discussion on each of these areas of development.

Each chapter begins with milestones for measuring development in that specific area, followed by suggestions for games and activities to promote development, and signs of possible problems so that you will know when to seek help. This is followed by a look at the role of pre-primary school, and how you should go about choosing a school.

In conclusion, there is a short chapter with guidelines on establishing whether your child is ready for school. This is not an official school-readiness test and it is not only directed at pre-primary children. By looking at the typical characteristics of normal toddlers from the age of three, you can systematically monitor your child's progress and intervene at an early stage if this seems necessary.

Enjoy your journey of discovery with your child, and allow him or her to set the pace. Bear in mind that your child's life cannot be a whirlwind of activity. Toddlers need quiet times as well as busy times, routine as well as challenges, and fun as well as more serious tasks in order to develop into truly balanced little people.

Play and toys

Play is invaluable in your child's development and forms the basis of all learning activities in her pre-school years. During the course of each day, she is involved in some form of play. This is part of being a child and there are few aspects of your child's development that cannot be associated with play. Not only does playing encourage development, it also reflects the level of your child's development.

When is a child playing?

When a child is attempting to reach a goal (for example to gain approval or acceptance), this kind of activity cannot really be called play, as the playful nature of the activity is relegated to the background. The activity becomes 'work' rather than play. If the child has no choice about participating in the activity, it also cannot be called play. And nobody can say that a child is 'playing' when she is clearly not enjoying the activity. When a child is passively watching someone else play, it cannot be said that she is playing either. Play, therefore, can generally be described as an activity from which a baby or child derives pleasure, and in which she is participating because she wishes to do so. Playing is something babies and children do because they enjoy it. Initially, a baby plays for no other reason than to have fun.

Jean Piaget, a Swiss psychologist, believed that from birth to two years, play is a repetition of the investigative activities children use to explore the world with their senses: they grasp, smell, taste, look and listen over and over until they have processed every piece of information. Once they can control a new object or process, they begin the next process of exploring, precisely because they have enjoyed the process of exploring and mastering so much.

As a parent, there is no need for you to fret about the purpose and meaning of play – rather enjoy the pleasure your child derives from play, and allow her to play because she enjoys it. The rest will automatically follow.

Play leads to growth and development

Just as your child grows and develops, her play also grows and develops. As her abilities and skills increase, she is able to include more and more activities and objects into her games. The best toy for a new-born baby is her mother – her favourite object to look at is her mother's face. She listens to her mother's voice, and enjoys her loving touch. When she is able to hold and handle objects, she will become interested in them. Eventually she will be sitting up and reaching for objects – shaking, rattling, putting it in her mouth, and exploring it in all kinds of ways.

When she learns that she can drop objects, she will delight in this activity. Once she begins to crawl, and later to walk, moving around will be her favourite pastime. She will be able to reach more objects and explore many things fully. Now she will begin to stack objects, and to knock them over. At the age of two she begins to understand the function of objects and the intentions of people. This leads to simple fantasy games in which she interprets the roles of the people around her. She pretends to drink out of a cup or to eat with a spoon, and through play these activities become established. At two a child also begins to draw others into her games.

If you play with your baby and make sure she has a variety of interesting objects to play with, you will certainly be stimulating her progress and development. But do not overwhelm her with activities and learning experiences – she also needs quiet times to assimilate what she has already experienced and learned, to make it her own, and to integrate it with other experiences and knowledge. A child needs new experiences, but these should be introduced gradually. It is very important that you allow your child to set her own pace. An overstimulated child can become tired, confused and irritable, and eventually be just as unhappy as a child who is bored and has nothing to do.

Characteristics of play

For your child, playing is a medium of discovery and creativity. It stimulates her thinking, language, and memory, and encourages planning, problem-solving, and exploring. Children's play has the following characteristics:

- Play does not follow rules – it is spontaneous.
- To a child, play is part of reality.
- Your child concentrates on the actual process of playing rather than on achieving something – on how the game is played rather than on the purpose of the game.
- The activity is dominated by the players.
- The activity requires the players to be actively involved.

The value of play

Play is a natural way in which your child explores and discovers – and eventually masters – the world around her. For that reason it is vitally important in the development of her abilities at all levels: her thinking and memory, language skills; mobility, hand- and foot-eye co-ordination; and her social and emotional maturity.

- Play is not only a means of learning, it is also a way of expressing herself. Through play, a child expresses how she sees and experiences her world.
- Play offers your child a safe environment in which she can dare and explore.
- Playing with other children develops a child's social skills. She learns to share, to be considerate toward others, and that she cannot always be the centre of attention.
- Play stimulates your child's emotional development and independence. She gradually learns to be independent and to make her own decisions.
- Play develops your child's creativity. The more imaginative her games, the more she will learn.
- Playful activities, such as running, climbing, scrambling, throwing a ball, picking up and carrying objects all contribute towards your child's physical development and help her to exercise control over her body.

- Playing is a way of getting rid of excess energy in a positive way.
- Play encourages a child's concentration and teaches her to order her thoughts and to plan activities.
- Through play, a child gathers information, which forms the basis for formal activities – for example, playing with blocks teaches her that two squares form a rectangle, and two triangles form a square.
- Playing provides many opportunities for problem-solving and teaches your child to take the initiative, to make use of what she already knows, and to integrate it with her life experiences.

Toys

Children do not need expensive and sophisticated toys. You may have seen the television advertisement of a one-year-old toddler playing with an empty cardboard box for hours. She climbs in and out, pushes it around, pulls it over her head, turns it upside down, picks it up and puts it down, and then starts all over again. Smaller boxes can be stacked or placed inside each other.

Old pots and pans with a wooden spoon or two are excellent drum sets, and plastic bowls with lids, in different shapes and sizes, are ideal for exercising deft little fingers. A large dish full of water with several plastic bowls that can float, an old funnel and a couple of empty cooldrink bottles will keep any little one busy for hours.

Most children enjoy playing in a sand box. Make sure there are enough spades, buckets, biscuit cutters, and so on for building sand castles, making mud cakes, or doing whatever your child's imagination leads her to try out. If you do not have a sand box in the garden, prepare a corner in the garden where she can bake mud cakes. Or buy a small, hard plastic swimming pool and fill it with building sand.

Stuff a strong plastic bag with crumpled newspaper (let your toddler help you), knot it and tie another bag around it to make it strong. This makes a lovely, inexpensive ball to kick or throw; your toddler will have good control over it, as it cannot roll away or break windows. And when it is worn out, you simply make another one.

When a child is playing happily, she will obviously get dirty and wet. Don't stop a game of discovery for this reason. It is easy enough to clean and dry a child when she has finished playing. It is much more difficult to rekindle a spirit of discovery once it has been dampened.

Shop toys

If you do buy toys or equipment for activities, consider the following:

- Pull and push toys
- Sit and ride tricycle
- Balls for rolling, kicking and catching
- A large ball a child can lie and roll on
- Bath-time toys: ducks, boats, bottles, plaric cups
- Building blocks in different sizes and shapes
- A soft toy or rag doll to cuddle
- Toys with shapes that fit into the same shaped openings, such as a shape board or a shape ball
- Bean or sand bags (for catching and balancing games; you can also make them – *see* page 39)
- Clay/plasticine or play dough
- Paint and paint brushes

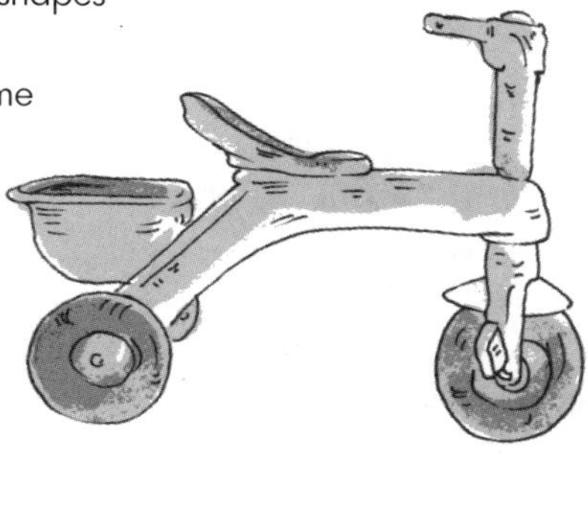

- Crayons (the thickness must be suitable for the child's age)
- A peg board
- Puzzles
- Glue and blunt-ended scissors
- Building toys, such as Duplo™ blocks for younger and Lego™ for older toddlers
- Musical instruments, such as a tambourine, bells, toy piano, cymbals
- If you specifically want to buy educational toys, make sure they are suitable for your child's age and level of development.

RECIPE FOR PLAY DOUGH

2 cups water	Bring all the ingredients to the boil.
1/2 cup salt	Remove from heat.
4 t cream of tartar	Stir in 2 cups of cake flour.
(or 1 T alun, from a chemist)	Knead well. The dough must not
2 T cooking oil	stick to your hands. Add more
food colouring	flour if necessary.

FINGER PAINT

See recipe on page 119. Younger toddlers, in particular, enjoy using finger paint since it is thicker and does not run.

MUD PAINT

Children of all ages enjoy playing with mud. In addition to making mud cakes, it is great fun to paint with mud. All you need to do, is supply the paper. Your toddler will make a mud mixture that will be suitable for paint, and create her own works of art.

CRAYONS

Buy crayons suitable for your child's age (thicker crayons for younger toddlers – *see* page 66).

PUZZLES

Buy puzzles appropriate to your child's age or ability (*see* page 43). The simplest puzzles consist of only two pieces. Allow your toddler to progress gradually to more pieces once she has mastered her current puzzles.

Rough and tumble

It is important that toddlers be allowed to play rough and to wrestle sometimes – this is how they let off steam, and a friendly tussle can't do any harm.

Just watch how baby animals learn their mobility skills – by bumping, climbing, tumbling, chasing and catching each other. If you have more than one cat or dog, you can be sure they also play like that.

Toddlers engaged in rough and tumble will giggle and laugh and shout while they play. The sounds will tell you when it's time to intervene. Don't intervene before it is necessary.

Development of the senses

Your baby's senses play an important role in his development, even before birth. For example, he can already hear vague sounds outside the uterus. When you talk to your unborn baby, or even read stories to him, he can hear you and soon learns to recognise your voice. Soft classical music has a soothing effect on the foetus, and he responds to loving touch when you stroke your stomach.

From the day he is born, your child begins to learn through his senses – they are the doors to his knowledge. His senses send signals to his brain, and his brain processes this information. The more information the senses send to the brain, the more information is processed and the better the brain develops. You are the one who must provide the stimulation for learning process.

Sight

Initially, your baby's sight is not well developed. He can vaguely make out things, but cannot focus clearly. At birth, he can only see about 20 to 30 cm ahead. Visual stimulation is therefore essential right from the beginning.

Babies prefer looking at stationary objects. They also prefer toys or objects in bright colours.

Your baby will gradually become interested in more complicated patterns, and as his vision develops, he will also begin to differentiate between colours. At two months, he can already distinguish between grey and other colours, and between red and green. In the first couple of months, your baby will also learn to follow objects with his eyes, and at three months his eyes begin to work together.

Encourage this development by holding an object in front of his face and slowly moving it to the right and to the left, so that he can follow it with his eyes.

What has all this to do with school-readiness – something still so far in the future? A lot. These exercises not only strengthen your infant's eye muscles, which he will eventually need to move his eyes over written words when he reads, but they also develop his visual perception (what he sees).

At an early age your baby already learns to observe simple shapes as something constant. He recognises his bottle and dummy at the age of three months – his excitement when he sees his bottle is proof of this.

He has a natural ability to make sense of what he sees, which is why he should be allowed to look at different shapes and objects in order to develop his perceptual ability. It is also important that he sees things from different positions or angles – while lying on his back or stomach, sitting in his chair, from the sling or papoose against your body, or from his pram.

This plays a crucial role in his development of spatial perception – where he is in relation to the world around him. At a young age, your infant will also perceive depth when he reaches towards or grabs objects. Depth perception will gradually teach him to be careful when he crawls, so that he will automatically stop when he crawls to the stairs, for example. The development of depth perception is essential for developing the ability to see three-dimensionally (what is in front or close up, what is behind and far away).

Hearing

Your new-born baby's hearing is better developed than his sight, and he recognises his mother's voice within the first week. He is tuned into sound almost immediately, and is particularly receptive to high-pitched sounds. The optimal development of his sense of hearing is crucial to your child's intellectual development. As he grows, his learning process depends more and more on hearing and listening. A child who is able to hear and listen well learns faster, makes fewer mistakes, and is less easily frustrated.

Taste, smell, and touch

With adults, sight and sound are the dominant senses, followed by touch, and then only taste and smell. With babies, however, touch, taste and smell are initially far more important. In fact, touch remains one of your infant's most important instruments for exploring right up to the time he goes to school. That is why he tries to touch everything within his reach, and puts every new object he discovers in his mouth.

Your infant fidgets and touches because it is his way of exploring the world around him.

Initially, your baby recognises you by your smell, before he recognises your face. He uses his sense of smell to identify people and objects while his eyes do not work together all that well.

A new-born baby has a complete set of taste glands. Although it takes a few years before these glands have fully developed, your baby will show a preference for something sweet, and his face will tell you when something is sour!

The table on pages 26-27 shows the milestones in the development of the various senses.

Activities and games to stimulate sensory development

Suitable games and activities to stimulate the development of the senses will of necessity be age related. At the age of 12 months sensory development is quite advanced. At this stage perceptual development becomes more important (see page 33).

New-born baby

Vary your baby's position when you put him down to sleep so that he can see the light from different directions. Change his 'view' regularly by holding him in such a way that he can look over your shoulder while you move around.

Hang a simple, brightly coloured mobile above his bed, about 26 cm from his eyes. It should not be shiny or move too much. Use blankets with different patterns and textures for his bed.

Sight	Hearing	Smell	Taste	Touch
New born				
▲Pupils react to light ▲Makes eye contact ▲Focuses on object 20-25 cm away ▲Turns head towards the light	▲Hears high-pitched sounds ▲Startled when he hears loud noise ▲Calms down with soothing sounds (voice or music) ▲Recognises mother's voice	▲Recognises mother's smell	▲Prefers sweet taste ▲Pulls a face when something tastes sour	▲Hands closed ▲Turns head and opens mouth when his cheek is touched ▲Uncontrolled hand movements in direction of sound/light ▲Fingers involuntary close around something placed in his hand
1 month				
▲Blinks at close object/bright light ▲Looks intently at mother's face ▲Eyes and head move together	▲Prefers higher pitched sounds (female voices) ▲Moves when he hears mother's voice			
3 months				
▲Eyes work/focus together ▲Distinguishes colours ▲Prefers moving objects and faces ▲Sees out of the corner of eyes (180 °)	▲Looks at you when you talk ▲Turns head towards sound	▲Responds to bad smells		▲No longer waves his arms in direction of light
4 months				
▲Distinguishes facial expressions ▲Immediately notices swinging object	▲Recognises voices besides mother's voice			
5 months				
▲Depth perception improves ▲Reaches out for objects he thinks he can touch	▲Responds to his own name			▲Hands open, reaches out to touch and grasp (voluntary) ▲Explores objects with his mouth

Sight	Hearing	Smell	Taste	Touch
6 months				
▲Changes body position to see better and controls the direction in which he is looking ▲Visually very aware and looks at objects further away	▲Immediately turns towards mother's voice at a distance ▲Shows understanding of emotions in mother's voice ▲Turns towards sounds from above/below ▲Recognises tunes			▲Transfers object from one hand to the other, but can't let go
8 months				
▲Can make out the size of an object from 65 cm away ▲Looks at a toy in his hands ▲Prefers looking at complicated objects	▲Can distinguish sounds ▲Recognises his name			▲Begins to stroke and prod objects with fingers
9 months				
▲Depth perception improves, does not crawl down stairs head first ▲Looks for objects he drops ▲Crawls or drags himself to toys	▲Recognises names of people and familiar objects ▲Responds to 'no' ▲Responds to one or two instructions		▲Accepts other tastes ▲Shows what he likes and dislikes	▲Uses his hands to explore objects ▲Can hold objects between thumb and forefinger ▲Laughs when he is tickled
12 months				
▲Responds to a smile ▲Follows fast-moving objects ▲Sight developed almost as much as an adult	▲Responds to simple instructions ▲Understands about six words			▲Strokes and taps with hands as loving touches ▲Turns objects around in his hand ▲Uses both hands

Talk to your baby while you are busy in the room. It is never too early to talk to your baby and to tell him about the world around him. Keep up a conversation while you are changing his bedding, or bathing and dressing him.

His eyes will follow you around the room and he will learn to listen to your voice. He will also systematically learn to relate movement, direction and distance with what he sees and hears. Play soft, soothing classical music while he sleeps.

Two to four months

Your baby will try to touch objects he sees. Encourage him by moving a brightly coloured toy, such as a rattle, in front of his eyes and put it in his hand, even when he can't hold it. In this way he will begin to combine information that his different senses send to his brain.

His toys should always be within his reach. Initially, he will try to touch them in an uncoordinated way. These actions stimulate not only his visual perception but also develop his muscle co-ordination. Change his position often during the course of the day – place him on his back, on his stomach, or upright in his chair so that he can see the world from different angles.

Move your baby's hands and feet while you play with him. He will begin to discover his body. Talk to your baby while you are busy with him. Tell him what you are doing and describe what you are busy with, for example 'Mommy is getting your nappy. I'm going to dry your bottom', or 'Here's your bottle'. Your baby will watch you and turn his head in the direction of your voice.

Four to six months

Now your baby is developing his ability to co-ordinate what he sees with what he does. He begins to reach out for objects. Encourage him to hold his bottle and allow him to put safe objects in his mouth. You are helping him to discover his own world by combining the information his different senses are sending to his brain.

Sing and dramatise nursery rhymes and songs. You are teaching your baby to co-ordinate what he hears with what he sees, as well as the movements of his body. He follows your movements with his eyes and will try to imitate your actions. Take your baby's hands and make clapping movements while you recite the rhyme 'Pat a cake' or 'Clap your handies'. Play the game 'Where is it? There it is!' by hiding an object behind your back, or holding your hand or a nappy in front of his eyes, then taking it away.

At this age babies like to bang objects together and to work out how the sound is made.

Let your infant play with objects made of different materials – allow him to feel and rub them so that he can develop a sense of texture.

Six to eight months

Hang a colourful mobile or other toy, such as a rattle, on a string where your baby can reach it and follow the moving object with his eyes.

He will keep his eyes focused on it and repeatedly try to grab it. This will encourage the development of his visual perception and concentration. Show him pictures of well-known objects and tell him what they are.

Roll a ball towards him that he can follow with his eyes. Talk to him while you are playing. Tell him 'This is a BALL. We are ROLLING the BALL'. Let your baby play on the rug with his toys on the floor, beyond his reach, so that he has to move towards it.

Allow your baby to play with pots and pans, or with toys that fit into each other. Again, talk to him while you play. Use words such as in, up, bigger, smaller, inside, outside, and so on. Place elastic bands with small bells loosely around his ankles and wrists. This will help him at an early age to develop eye-hand and eye-foot co-ordination, and listening skills.

Your baby will also enjoy hide-away games with his toys. Place a toy behind your back or under the rug while he is watching and ask him where it is. This develops his visual memory.

By throwing or dropping toys and picking them up (or indicating that you must pick it up!), he is developing an awareness of weight and space. Try to hide your impatience and encourage him with a smile by picking up the object until he indicates that he has had enough.

Eight to twelve months

At this stage, your infant can play with objects that consist of more than one part. Give him toys and objects that he can manipulate – for example something that makes a noise when he presses it, or when he drags it behind him. A simple xylophone will also give him a lot of pleasure.

Allow him to discover the kitchen cupboards – saucepans and plastic containers are safe to play with, even if it leaves the kitchen in a mess!

Movement, crawling or pulling himself forward with his arms, and then walking, now form a large part of your child's play activities. Let him move in and out of places on his own. He will like to crawl under a chair or coffee table. Leave him and allow him to get out by himself.

He must learn to experience his own size in relation to other objects and how to get himself out of problem situations. Talk to him while he is busy discovering and develop his language skills by telling him about direction, size, movement, and so on. When he has crawled under a chair, explain to him that he must crawl backwards to get out, and that he cannot crawl out as he came in.

Signs of problems

Serious problems, such as blindness, are usually identified during the first few weeks after birth. It may take longer to discover less serious problems. If your child is lagging behind according to the milestones, get professional help. The following can be signs of problems:

- Your child appears not to see you.
- At six months your baby is still squinting and cannot focus his eyes.
- Physical signs, such as a drooping eyelid.
- Your infant constantly crawls or bumps into objects.

Serious hearing problems will probably also be noticed at an early stage because it will quickly become clear if your child is not responding to sound. Partial deafness will be much more difficult to identify. If you think your child is not hearing well enough, get professional help. The following may be signs of problems:

- Your baby is not startled by loud sounds.
- Your baby responds when he sees you, but not when he hears you.
- Your baby, at six months, still consistently turns in the wrong direction when he tries to establish where a sound is coming from.
- After 18 to 24 months, your baby is still making no effort to talk.

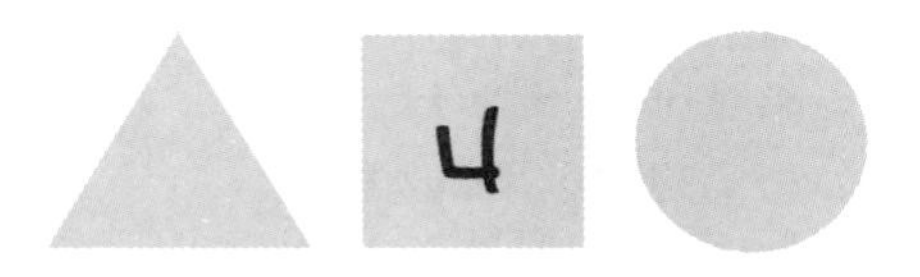

Perceptual development

Perception is the meaning the brain gives to messages received by means of the sensory nerves. Your baby sees a chair, and her brain tells her it is a chair. She hears you laugh, and her brain tells her it is you who are laughing. Perceptual development is therefore more than the development of the senses – it is the development of the ability to combine, recognise and classify the information the senses gather. Perception is therefore a sensory and a mental process.

As far as school-readiness is concerned, satisfactory development of visual and auditory perception is crucial. Visual perception is needed for colouring in, drawing, writing and reading. Auditory perception is the foundation of language development, listening and learning skills.

Visual perception

Visual perception is your child's ability to interpret, identify and categorise what she sees correctly. Her brain must be able to give meaning to what her eyes see. Why is visual perception so important? Most of our contact with our environment occurs through hearing and seeing. Visual and auditory perception are therefore essential in order to understand our environment. A baby learns to know and understand her environment through visual perception. For example, she learns that objects with a certain shape are called chairs, that other objects are called beds, that a ball is round and a table rectangular, that a car is bigger and a pencil smaller than she is.

When your child starts school, accurate visual perception will enable her to learn to read, write and do mathematics, and to tackle any other task that requires recognising and expressing symbols. With the right stimulation, the development of this ability occurs mainly between the ages of three to seven years. For school-readiness, we have to distinguish between the following important aspects of visual perception:

- **Visual discrimination**: your child's ability to distinguish visually between objects, and to observe the differences and similarities. She must understand what she sees, and classify this information.
- **Visual memory**: your child's ability to remember what she has seen.
- **Perception of shapes**: your child must recognise the shapes of objects, and know that something that is far away from her looks smaller than it actually is.
- **Visual analysis and synthesis**: your child's ability to see a pattern as a unit, to break it up into its different parts, and to put it together again.

Milestones in the development of visual perception

The development of your child's visual perception begins the day she is born. Every visual experience is part of the process of practising her visual perception in order to be ready for school when the time comes. You must be involved in this process from the beginning by ordering your child's environment and playing visual games with her. In this way, you will be contributing towards developing her visual sense, and laying a firm foundation for good visual perception. She must learn to use both eyes to see at reading distance as well as from further away, to understand what she sees, and to pay attention to one object without ignoring others. These visual skills help your child to understand and use what she sees.

One year to 24 months

- ▲ Your baby uses both hands; she looks first and then touches (12-14 months).
- ▲ She begins to look at simple pictures (14-16 months).
- ▲ She often holds toys and other objects very close to her eyes when studying them (14-18 months).
- ▲ She points to objects or people while using single words, such as 'dere', 'ta', 'look', 'see' (14-18 months).

- She looks at pictures of animals in books and identifies them by making the animal sounds (16-18 months).
- She smiles when seeing a popular toy, object or person. She is able to look without touching (20-24 months).

TWO TO THREE YEARS

- She likes to watch the movements of, for example, an egg beater or mixer, or the washing in the washing machine (24-28 months).
- Considerable visual discovery occurs and she can control her walking and climbing.
- She looks at her own hand while she scribbles with crayons (26-30 months).
- She watches other children and imitates them (30-36 months).
- She begins to 'read' and colour in pictures in books (34-38 months).

THREE YEARS

- She holds her head and eyes close to a book when paging through it.
- She can distinguish between a round and a square block.
- She can close her eyes when asked, and can wink one eye.
- She can draw a vertical and horizontal line.
- She recognises the basic colours – red, yellow, green and blue – and can sort blocks according to these colours.
- She can distinguish between big and small.
- She can recognise pictures in a book.
- She can make a simple puzzle with two to four pieces.
- She recognises people and knows their names.

THREE AND A HALF YEARS

- She recognises basic shapes, such as a triangle, circle, and square, and can fit it into a shape sorter.
- She can sort according to size, and choose the biggest and smallest of a variety of objects.
- She recognises more than only the basic colours, and can match almost all the colours.
- She recognises objects used in the house in magazines and advertisements.
- She can build a puzzle with six to eight pieces.

Four years

- ▲ She can match more difficult shapes, such as a rectangle, oval and semi-circle.
- ▲ She can trace shapes and distinguish between them, and match similar shapes, for example, two triangles to make a square.
- ▲ She can name most of the colours.
- ▲ She knows the difference between 1, 2 and 3, and less and more.
- ▲ She can point out different objects in a book and find specific toys in her toy box.
- ▲ She can build a puzzle with six to 15 pieces.
- ▲ She can remember the names of three to four familiar objects set out on a tray.

Four and a half years

- ▲ Your toddler can use her eyes and hands together with increasing skill (hand-eye co-ordination).
- ▲ She can trace a cross and slanting lines.
- ▲ She knows all the colours.
- ▲ She sees the detail in illustrations that do not directly relate to the story.
- ▲ She can build a puzzle with 15 to 20 pieces.
- ▲ She can remember the names of five items on a tray.

Five years

- ▲ She can observe her own body size and compare it with, for example, that of her father.
- ▲ She can point out an object in the centre.
- ▲ She can name all the colours and the shades as well. She can also arrange colours according to shades.
- ▲ She can find hidden objects in a picture.
- ▲ She can build a puzzle with 20 to 30 pieces if the picture is simple.
- ▲ She can name six objects set out on a tray.
- ▲ She can roll and move her eyes in an expressive way.
- ▲ She can draw pictures and colour in inside the lines.
- ▲ She can cut out pictures quite well and glue them down.

- Visually, she is aware and observant, and can talk about people, objects and places she has seen.
- She shows increasing interest in new objects and places.

FIVE AND A HALF YEARS

- She can distinguish between a square and a rectangle.
- She applies her perception of shape to objects, for example a saucer is round, a book is rectangular, a facecloth is square, and so on.
- She can fold a square piece of paper into a triangle.
- She can perceive that something is far away or close by, for example an aeroplane in the sky is smaller than the one on the ground.
- She can trace her name.
- She can trace figures.
- She can play card games such as 'Snap'.
- She can follow a pattern to make a picture with mosaic blocks or on a peg board with the help of a pattern.
- She can complete a puzzle with more than 30 pieces.

SIX YEARS

- She can draw and name all the shapes, and knows the differences as well.
- She knows all the primary and secondary colours, and knows that if you mix yellow and red you get orange.
- She can match letters and figures. She can also match three-letter words, even though she cannot read.
- She can match halves and quarters, for example make a circle with two semi-circles.

Activities and games to encourage visual perception

The development of visual skills is an essential part of school-readiness. You can encourage and promote it with easy activities and games. Keep the milestones in mind and address backlogs in the development of your child's visual perception at an early stage.

If necessary, get professional help from an occupational therapist. Also use the milestones when you choose activities and games. Make a point of thinking creatively, and use as many every-day, routine activities as you can find to stimulate each level of your child's development. Every routine task that you can turn into a game becomes an opportunity for learning, and gradually your child will realise that it is fun to learn.

Encourage your child from the beginning to acquire good visual habits. Good habits that are learned at an early stage will have a positive effect on her visual perception when she is at school.

Good lighting is very important, as well as the right sitting position when she sits at her little desk or table to draw. Encourage her to rest her eyes between drawing activities and to move around. In most cases, this happens naturally because your toddler's attention span is still short.

Two years

Help your child to develop her visual memory by making **hide-and-seek games** systematically more difficult. Send her to fetch a specific toy: 'Please go and fetch the red ball in the basket.'

Change the place where you keep specific toys in her room. If her blue rabbit usually lies on her bed, for example, move it to the bedside table. Tell her the rabbit is going to sit on the bedside table today, and make sure she sees you putting it there. Later in the day, send her to fetch the rabbit.

Show your child **pictures** in story books and discuss them with her. Ask her what or who she saw in the pictures.

When you drive in the car, or go for a walk, point out certain things, such as a dog, or birds, or other children. When you are home, ask her what she saw, and let her tell her father about it.

Develop her abstract thought by pointing out **differences**. Show her big and small dogs, big and small houses, and so on.

Three years

Let your child carry her own glass of milk or cooldrink, but don't fill the glass to the top. Tell her to be careful and to try not to spill it. At this age, children still trip up and spill milk or cooldrink, but that is common. Teach them to dry it up themselves when they have made a mess.

Give your toddler a **blackboard** and chalk and let her draw while standing. Allow her to draw her own pictures, even if they are only scribbles. It is a valuable exercise. Also let her draw on a large piece of paper on the floor or at a table. Give her crayons, a pencil, or make paint in one colour for variation. Allow her to express her own creativity.

Do not force her to colour in inside the lines or to draw the way you draw (*see* page 109 for more details about creativity, how to stimulate your child's creative development and general milestones in the development of drawing skills).

Let your child play with **building blocks** and **construction toys** such as Duplo™ and Lego™ as much as possible. She will enjoy playing with cotton reels, pill boxes, left-over pieces of wood and empty plastic bottles, especially in sand and water. Allow her to make a big mess. Mud can be washed off and the learning opportunities are endless. She will also enjoy playing with simple puzzles and a peg board.

FOUR YEARS

Make a **bean bag** for your child to throw and catch – it is easier to catch than a ball and can be used for a great variety of games and activities. Bake dried beans or mealie cernels for 30 minutes in a pre-heated oven (180 °C/ 350 °F) or put it in the microwave for 3-5 minutes on High to prevent mites. Leave to cool off. Make the bag of strong fabric, such as bull denim or calico, about 10 cm x 20 cm. Fill with beans and stitch the open seam. Make plain as well as multi-coloured bean bags.

Let your child experiment on her own with the bean bag so that she can learn to control it, and to catch it. First stand close to her when you throw the bag so that she can succeed in catching it. Teach her to look at the bag so that she can catch it. As her co-ordination improves, stand further away. Teach her how to throw the bag.

Place the laundry basket or a cardboard box about one meter from her and let her try to throw the bag in the basket or box. For this game, you can also use the home-made ball (*see* page 19). As your child's skill improves, move the basket or box further away.

Let your child throw things at a **target**. Place empty coffee tins in a row and let her try to topple them with the bean bag. Or place the coffee tins about half a meter away from each other and let her use her foot to push the bag around and between the tins without knocking them over.

FIVE TO SIX YEARS

One can only see where there is light. Darken a room and shine a torch on specific objects. Ask your toddler to describe what she sees. Play other torch and **light games** with her. Show her the shadows when you shine the torch on an object, and show her her own shadow during the day. Play **shadow games**. Show her how to make animals with her hands, and let her discover whether her shadow follows her upstairs or around a corner.

Show your child **transparent** things. Turn window cleaning into a game. On a rainy day, when the windows are misted up, wipe a small window so that she can look outside. Let her name all the things she can see through it. Point out liquids in different kinds of bottles, and reflecting surfaces such as mirrors, spoons, pools of water, and so on.

Place objects in a large glass container filled with water so that she can see how they change under water. Let your child look through a telescope and at a small object or insect through a magnifying glass. A **magnifying glass** will provide hours of fun and learning opportunities. Let your child play with an old camera to learn how to view the world around her selectively and with discrimination.

Spend time in **nature** with your child. Gather autumn leaves in different shapes, or shells or pebbles, and ask her to arrange them according to shape, size or colour.

Playing cards also keep toddlers busy for hours. They can sort them according to colour, numbers, pictures, and so on.

All the games and activities mentioned above can be adjusted for older toddlers and still present a challenge and stimulate their development. Let your child lead you and adjust her activities according to the level of her development.

There are also useful games and activities to help the development of finer aspects of visual perception.

Games for the development of visual memory

You can play this game with toddlers as young as two to three because it can be adjusted according to their age. Use three items for a three year old, and four for a four year old. Place three (or four or five) of your child's favourite toys in front of her. Say 'I'm going to hide a toy behind my back and you must guess which one it is. Take a good look at what is here.' Let her name the toys lying in front of her. 'Now shut your eyes tightly while I hide one of the toys. Which one did I hide?'

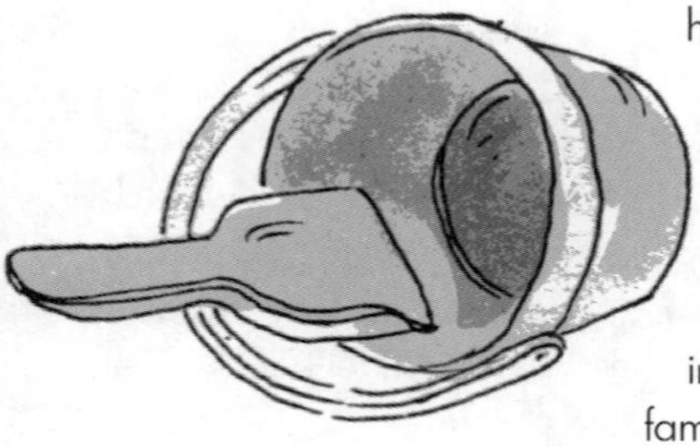

You can also play the game with coloured blocks. 'Which colour block did I take away?' and so on.

Place a number of objects on a tray. Begin again with three, four or five according to her age. Use objects your child is familiar with, for example a spoon, mug, apple, or toys. Tell her to look at them and name them. Throw a towel over them and let her name them again. Increase the number of items according to your child's progress. Six items are sufficient for a six year old.

Make a simple **figure** with matches and ask your child to do the same. It must be easy to begin with and become progressively more difficult.

Your child must be successful and enjoy the game, otherwise she will become discouraged.

Use **story books** or any other **pictures** from magazines, for example a picture of a family by the sea or in a house. Show it to her and ask her to tell you what she sees. Take the picture away and ask what she saw. Ask about the colour of the little boy's shirt, or what the girl was holding in her hands.

When you are driving in your car, point out things along the road, for example a dog on the pavement, or a car passing. When you have passed it, ask what colour the dog or car was. Teach your child to really observe things and not merely to look at them.

Cut out pictures of five kinds of food, five pieces of furniture, five kinds of toys, and five clothing items from magazines. Allow her to look at the pictures for one minute, take them away and let her name the things she sees.

Next, arrange the pictures in their categories and ask her to look at them again. Take them away and let her name them. Because she stores the pictures in her mind in categories, she will be able to remember more.

Make this game more difficult by showing the pictures arranged at random, and then ask her to name everything that can be eaten, or played with, and so on.

Games for the development of visual discrimination

Give your child a drawer full of cutlery, and let her arrange them according to kind: all the knives together, spoons together, teaspoons together, and so on. Do the same with a few plastic containers. Let her put the round ones together, then the square ones, then the rectangular ones, and so on. This game can also be played with building blocks. Ask your toddler to arrange the blocks according to shape or colour. Older toddlers can be asked to arrange them according to shape and colour.

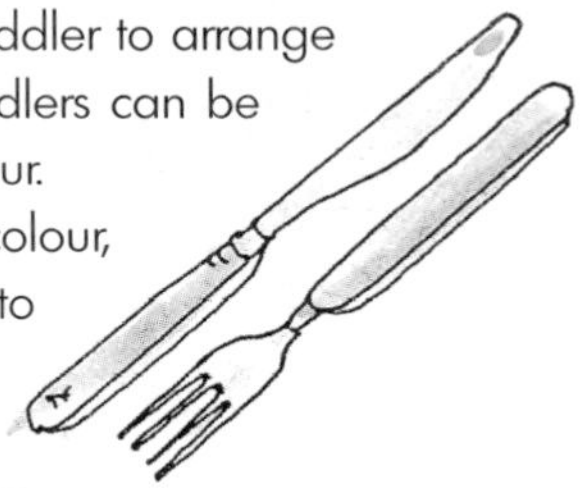

A tin of buttons can also be sorted according to colour, size and shape. When your child sorts according to colour and size, ask her to put all the buttons with holes in one tin, and those with a shank in another tin. Then give her buttons of the same shape and size, but with two or four holes, and let her sort them according to the number of holes. Zippers can also be fun. Let your child sort them according to their length, colours and kind: rough or smooth, metal or plastic.

Let her sort her own toys: all the blocks in one container, all the cars in another. All the large books must be packed in the bottom shelf, and the smaller ones in the top shelf.

Play '**I spy with my little eye**' with objects in the house. Use colours and shapes for variation.

Your **vegetable rack** can become an irresistible source of games. Let your child sort the vegetables according to kind, colour, shape and smell. Teach her about similarity and difference, that they are all vegetables even though they have different shapes, colours and tastes.

When you walk in the garden or a park, let your child show you all the yellow, red or white flowers, or the flowers with their faces up or down, or that look the same (the same kind) even though the colours are different.

For your older toddler you can cut out magazine pictures of different products. Paste them on cardboard to make them sturdy, or use as is. Let your child **sort** them in different categories, for example everything that can be eaten, that tastes sweet or sour, what we can drink, or use in the bathroom or kitchen, which furniture goes into which room ... the possibilities are endless.

Games for developing perception of shapes

Let your child make geometric shapes with her body or limbs. Say, 'Let's play you are a triangle, a circle, a square', and so on. Or let your child walk around the house and point out any rectangle, square or triangle she sees (doors, windows, and so on). Give her clues.

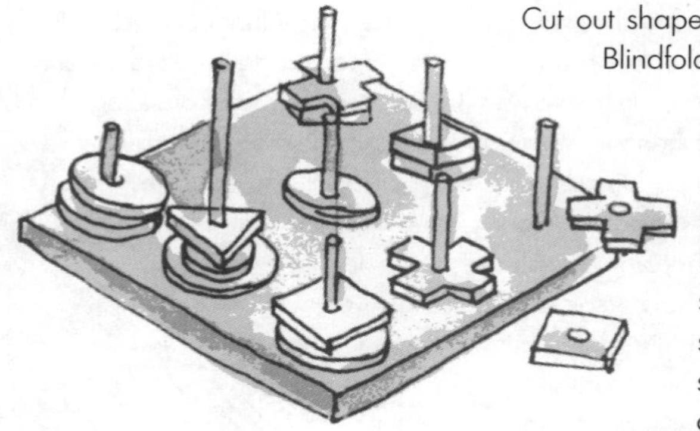

Cut out shapes from thick cardboard. Blindfold your child with a soft cloth and ask her to feel the shapes one by one and guess which shape she has in her hand. Let her use the cardboard shapes to build other shapes, for example a square with two triangles, a house with a square and a triangle.

Show her what she can do with the shapes, and allow her to experiment for herself.

Let your child help you bake cookies and press out dough in different shapes.

Games for the development of visual analysis and synthesis

Toddlers between four and five years can begin with activities and games for visual analysis and synthesis as long as they are two-dimensional. At the age of six they can begin working with three-dimensional **templates**.

Arrange a pattern with blocks or tiles. For example, begin with blocks: one green, one red, and one green block. Let your child repeat the pattern. Once she masters this, use more blocks, for example one green, two yellow, one green. Vary the pattern and use different shapes.

Arrange shapes and patterns with sticks or matches. Teach her that a pattern is made up of shapes that are repeated.

While you are busy in the kitchen, arrange some vegetables in a pattern, for example one potato, one onion, one potato, one onion. Let her repeat the pattern. You could also use cutlery: one knife, one spoon, one knife, one spoon. Make the pattern more difficult once she masters one pattern, for example two potatoes, one onion, two potatoes, one onion, or one spoon, two forks, one knife, one spoon, two forks, one knife.

You could also use the cardboard shapes you made. Arrange them to form patterns and let your child do the same. As she progresses, make the pattern slightly more complicated, for example by placing the square, rectangle or triangle at an angle.

Build **puzzles**. Begin at an early age with two-piece puzzles where one half fits into the other half to complete the picture. Initially, the pictures must be very simple with few details.

As your child progresses, use more difficult puzzles with four, eight, and up to 24 pieces. Take note of the picture depicted. A very busy picture, with lots of detail, but few pieces, is more difficult than a puzzle with a simple picture and more pieces.

Play '**Finish the picture**'. Draw half a face, flower, house or cat and ask her to finish the picture.

Let your child complete simple patterns on a **peg board**. Teach her to work systematically according to a pattern from a template, just as she imitated your patterns with cutlery and vegetables.

Signs of problems

Take your child to an optician if you are at all worried about her sight. The following may be signs of a problem:

- Your child's eyes are crossed at times. With some toddlers, one eye turns to the inside, especially when their eyes are tired.
- Your child cannot follow your finger smoothly with her eyes – the movement of her eyes is uneven.
- Her eyes are red and itchy, and she rubs them a lot.
- She is oversensitive to light.
- She blinks her eyes excessively and screws them tightly.
- Her eye-lids are red and caked up.
- She often gets styes.
- She has unusually limp eyelids.
- Her eyes run when she colours in or pages through books.
- Her eye-hand co-ordination lags behind that of her peer group.
- She struggles to imitate your body movements.
- She often falls over objects because she does not see them.
- She falls off her bicycle.

Auditory perception

Auditory perception is your child's ability to attach meaning to the sounds she hears. She learns systematically that certain combinations of sounds have specific meaning and convey information in this way. Auditory perception is essential for your child's language development, and, in turn, language development is essential for her intellectual development. For school-readiness, we distinguish between the following important aspects of auditory perception:

- **Auditory discrimination**: your child's ability to distinguish between sounds that sound similar and those that sound different, in other words, to hear similarities and differences. Sounds may also differ as far as sound intensity is concerned (hard and soft), pitch (high and low), duration (long and short), and interval.
- **Auditory memory**: your child's ability to remember a series of related or unrelated sounds and repeat it in the sequence presented. This is crucial to language development. To remember the sequence of sounds in a word, and words in a sentence, is essential to understanding language. The development of your child's auditory memory has a direct influence on her reading and spelling ability.

- **Auditory analysis and synthesis**: your child's ability to break up the sounds of a word on one hand, and to form a word by combining sounds on the other hand.
- **Auditory foreground-background perception**: your child's ability to focus her attention on specific sounds at a specific time, for example her mother's voice, even when there are sounds in the background.

To develop these skills, your child's hearing must be well developed, and he must be good at paying attention and distinguishing between sound patterns. Your role in the development of these skills cannot be emphasised enough.

From the beginning, talk to your child. Make her aware of sounds around her. Teach her the names of everyday objects in and around the house. Use descriptive words and teach her to form associations (see page 79-82, Milestones for language development).

Games and activities for the development of auditory perception

Because auditory perception plays such an important role in language development and language acquisition, the suggestions for games and activities to promote language development are devoted to auditory perception (*see* page 82).

Signs of hearing problems

Toddlers often suffer from chronic ear infections that can impede their hearing. If you suspect that your toddler's hearing is not a hundred per cent, get professional help (ask your general practitioner for a referral).

Be on the lookout for the following signs of possible hearing problems (*see* also page 31):

- Language problems, for example poor vocabulary, wrong pronunciation of some letters such as m and n, b and d, and d and t because your child cannot hear the difference.
- Your child does not respond when you talk to or call her.
- Your child cannot follow simple instructions.
- Your child turns the radio or television on very loud in order to hear. She will also sit very close, with her ear almost against the radio.
- Your child speaks very loudly.
- Your child does not respond to the telephone or doorbell.

From the outset, make a point of looking your child in the eye when you talk to her. Teach her first to listen and then to respond when you give instructions.

Make sure she knows what you expect from her. Let her repeat what you have said – in this way you will know that she has listened. Never give your child instructions in passing; it is most likely that she will not 'hear'. If you speak to her in the right way, she will learn to listen the first time every time. You will be helping her from a young age to acquire good listening skills.

Spatial perception

Spatial perception is linked to visual discrimination. This is the ability to identify small differences and similarities. These differences are often of a spatial nature.

A new-born baby does not know where she ends and the world begins, and looks mainly at her hands and feet and objects close to her eyes – she has no spatial perception. This ability to observe the position of objects in relation to herself and in relation to other objects, develops at a rapid pace.

At five months your baby is already systematically looking around her and examining all kinds of objects. Between six and eight months she begins to search for something she has dropped, and often picks it up herself. At 18 months to two years most infants enjoy playing with a sit and ride with which they can change direction, they can push a wheelbarrow, look for objects hidden away, and later, drag an object behind them. They are also aware of their own position and movement while they push, pull or search for something.

At three years your child makes recognisable drawings, although many elements are still missing and nothing is according to scale. For example, a person will consist of a large head with a couple of lines for the legs. At four years she begins to allow for your perspective when she explains something that has happened (before this age she would describe everything as if she was the centre without any realisation that your perspective may be different). She can also explain to you where you should look for something. She knows that she is sitting on a chair at the table, that the table is on the rug, and the rug under the table, and that the tricycle is in front of the ball and the ball behind the tricycle.

Five-year-olds duck, dive and cut corners when running or chasing their friends. Their drawings have more slanting lines, but a chimney will be at an angle with the roof. At the age of six to seven your child can point in the direction of places she cannot see. Her drawings contain more detail, are already almost according to scale, and show that she can distinguish between foreground and background.

Games for the development of spatial perception

From the age of six months you can entertain your child for long periods by picking up objects she throws down. Encourage this, even if it tests your patience! Invest in a strong sit and ride tricycle (toddler's motorbike), which is made of hard plastic, as soon as your child can walk. Not only is it good for the development of motor skills, it also helps with a sense of direction.

Between the ages of 18 months and two years, children begin to enjoy any hide-and-seek games. Make the games systematically more complicated. Play with building blocks or a soft toy such as a teddy bear. Keep up a conversation with your child while you play. Ask her, 'Where is your teddy? Is it ON the table? Is it IN FRONT OF the bed? Is it UNDER the blanket?' Make sure she had a wagon or wheelbarrow to push around. Play-dough and simple puzzles can give a child hours of pleasure, and from four years they really enjoy sand and water games. While your child plays, you must talk to her and help her to absorb concepts.

Encourage older toddlers who enjoy running around and climbing on jungle gyms to tell you what they are doing, for example, 'I'm climbing UP, I'm climbing DOWN, I'm climbing OVER, I'm crawling THROUGH,' or, when they crawl through tunnels, 'I'm crawling FORWARD, I'm climbing BACKWARDS'. Make a game of shapes by letting her run in circles, squares or triangles. Remember, though, that play is only play when your child enjoys what she is doing. Do not force her to continue when she has had enough or wants to do something else.

Foreground-background observation

To ensure the best possible observation, you have to pay attention to whatever you are observing. The human brain is capable of selecting and attending to a certain amount of the information the senses send to the brain. At a specific point in time, this selected information forms a clearly defined foreground of what you observe, while the rest of the information forms a less-defined background.

Foreground-background observation can therefore be described as the ability to put the objects that are being attended to at a specific moment in the foreground, and to put things that are less important at that moment in the background.

It is important that your child's foreground-background observation is well developed when she starts school, so that she can focus her attention.

Games and activities for the development of foreground-background observation

After reading a story to your child, ask her to look for something **specific** in a picture, for example, 'Where is the bird, where is the red flower, where is the rabbit's eyes?' and so on.

Older toddlers can look for hidden objects in a picture.

Play '**Snap**' with your child, using ordinary playing cards.

Help her to make **scrap books** of specific subjects. Give her magazines to page through to look for pictures about the different subjects, to cut them out and paste them in her scrap books.

Play '**Find the letter**'. Write a large letter on a piece of paper or in a book. Ask your child to look for more letters like that one in magazines, and to circle them.

5

Development of movement

All babies are born with an innate need for movement, which they discover in a spontaneous way. To a baby, the need for movement is as fundamental as eating and sleeping. The skills that enable your baby to move are called motor skills. Large activities, such as crawling and walking, depend on gross muscle development; while smaller movements, such as the hand movements that enable a child to draw or fasten buttons, depend on fine muscle development and co-ordination. Gross muscle development occurs before fine muscle development and co-ordination. The development of both these skills is essential for school-readiness, as well as for your child's later progress at school.

Order of development

If you know how your child's brain develops, as well as how the gross and fine muscles that control his movements develop, you will know what to expect at which age, and you can involve him in games and activities that match his abilities.

The development of motor skills takes place from the head downwards, spreading from the body to the limbs: a baby must first learn to lift his head before he can turn round; he can first control his arms, then his legs; and he will first kick with his legs before moving his toes.

A new-born baby's muscles are weak, his bones are soft and his nervous system is not fully formed or developed. Within the next 18 months his muscles become stronger, his bones harden and the parts in his brain that control movement develop fully. The most important skills your infant masters within the first 18 months is to move from place to place, and to reach for and grasp objects. The rate of development is largely determined by genetic factors, but if you encourage your infant to use his muscles, he will develop faster.

It is very important to note the order of development. The development of movement and co-ordination is predictable and occurs in an orderly manner: your baby will probably not sit up before he can turn himself round, or walk before he can crawl.

Although some children never crawl, they do substitute this activity with something else, like pulling themselves forward or shifting on their bottoms before they start walking.

Milestones in gross motor development

Use these as guidelines, and obtain professional help if you suspect that your child is not showing sufficient progress.

New-born baby to ten weeks

Your baby turns his head sideways only and makes spontaneous movements with his arms and legs. He also likes to stretch. Initially, he has no control over these movements. At eight weeks he can keep his head still when you hold him under the arms.

Three to eight months

Between three and six months a baby has more control over his body. He can lift his head and chest when lying on his tummy or back, stretch his arms out and roll over onto his tummy or back. He can turn in all directions and slowly learns to sit by himself. At six to eight months he can sit by himself, and roll over from his back onto his tummy. He can turn around to get hold of a toy. Some babies are quite content just to sit, play with their toys and watch the world. Other babies, once they have learned to roll over, will move from one place to another without help.

Nine to twelve months

At about nine months, your baby will start crawling or pulling himself forward. Some babies use their legs to move into a sitting position, while others combine shifting and rolling in order to move. He will start pulling himself up against the furniture, and shift sideways while holding onto something. Between 10 and 12 months he will take a few steps when you hold his hands, and at 12 months he will be able to stand by himself. Some infants begin to walk at this age, but they are in the minority.

THIRTEEN TO EIGHTEEN MONTHS

Most babies start walking between 13 and 15 months. They walk with legs apart and arms in the air. At 18 months they can walk backwards and forwards, and run, although they will still fall quite often. Your child can now move to and sit on a small chair by himself.

THIRTEEN TO EIGHTEEN MONTHS

He will be walking better, and drop his arms when he walks. He will climb onto bigger chairs and then climb down again. He can climb stairs if you hold his hand, with both feet on one step before ascending the next one, or attempt the stairs by crawling up by himself. He can ride on his sit-and-ride tricycle and does not lose his balance when he bends down from a standing position to pick up something from the floor. He can kneel without falling over.

Two and a half years

He can aim a ball when throwing it, and kick without losing his balance. He can also squat without losing his balance. If you hold his hand, he can take a few steps on a narrow wall (balancing bar). He can stand on one leg for about one second, hop on one leg three times on the same place, and jump over a low obstacle with both feet. He can play on a simple jungle gym, and push a toy wheelbarrow or wagon.

Three years

He can ride a tricycle. His movements are rhythmic and he can hop and jump. He enjoys ball games and catches a large ball with stiff arms.

He can hop five times on his dominant foot on one spot and three times on the other foot. He can stand on one leg for three seconds and walk heel-toe, heel-toe.

Three and a half years

He can stand on one leg for five seconds and cover a distance of three metres jumping on one leg. He alternates feet when ascending steps, and does not hold onto the railings. He can run backwards, turn around sharply, stop suddenly without falling, and hop and skip.

He can jump with both feet together, and bends his legs when he lands. He can throw a ball at a target and is comfortable playing on a jungle gym.

Four years

He can stand on one leg for seven seconds. He can jump backwards, climb up the steps of a slide on his own, and swing by himself. A ball of any size becomes a favourite toy and he can catch a large ball thrown from a short distance. He can kick and bounce a large ball, and throw a tennis ball.

Four and a half years

He can stand on one leg for nine seconds, walk four steps on a low wall (balancing bar), heel-toe, without falling off. He hops very well, alternating legs. He does somersaults, loves jumping on a trampoline, rides a tricycle, and can learn to swim, rollerskate, and do ballet or dancing.

Five years

Your toddler can run with light steps, much like an adult, and stand on one leg without difficulty (10-12 seconds). He can now walk forwards, backwards and sideways on a narrow wall (balancing bar). He can walk on his toes for five steps and jump six metres on one leg without using the other leg for support. If you bounce the ball at him, he will catch it, and he can hit a ball on a rope with a bat ('swing ball').

He can catch a bean bag with one hand, kick a rolling ball, and dribble a ball. His motor movements are rhythmic.

Five and a half years

Some toddlers can already ride a bicycle at this age, but will still fall off at times. Your toddler can march to the beat of music and learn simple dance steps. He can walk on his heels. He is skillful with a ball and can bounce it and catch it with two hands.

Six years

His alternates his feet when he hops, and can skip with a skipping rope. He walks heel-toe on a balancing bar effortlessly. Your toddler can stand on one leg with eyes closed for eight seconds, and with open eyes for 15 seconds.

He can do two or more somersaults after each other and throw bean bags in the air and catch them again.

Signs of gross motor development problems

Low muscle tone means that the natural tension in your child's muscles is not high enough. This makes him very floppy, and it will be more difficult for him to execute movements than for other babies. Such a problem can usually be diagnosed at the age of four to six months.

How will you know something is wrong?

- If at three months your baby is still so floppy that you are afraid to handle him.
- If at three months your baby cannot hold his head up when you hold him upright.
- If at three months your baby cannot lift his head when he is lying on his tummy.
- If at four months he is not reaching out to grasp objects.
- If at three to four months your baby is not making eye contact.
- If at three to four months your baby is not responding to sounds.
- If your baby sucks and drinks poorly, easily chokes on milk, and the milk runs out of his mouth.

Games and activities for development of gross motor skills

Be attentive to your infant's progress from the very beginning, and provide a stimulating but safe environment for him, with **a lot of interaction**. In this way you will help him towards school-readiness through play.

Research has shown that the development of motor skills in babies cannot be significantly speeded up by 'instruction' and that natural maturing at this early stage is more important than 'instruction'. What is important, however, is that your baby should have sufficient space for movement to practise the skills he acquires naturally.

His environment should also stimulate his natural curiosity to investigate and explore his surroundings. Therefore, your role as a parent is to provide this space for movement and stimulation, and to constantly encourage your infant when he attempts something. He will learn that his efforts elicit a positive response in you, and this will make him want to try again.

Once your infant, with his endless curiosity about everything and everybody around him, begins to crawl and then to walk, he will be embarking on a huge quest, constantly exploring his surroundings and his own abilities. He will develop new skills and be on the lookout for new challenges all the time. From now on he will enjoy playing games that test his motor skills. He will begin running, climbing and clambering.

Don't constantly warn him about hurting himself when he falls off something he has clambered onto – this will hinder his development, and make him unnecessarily afraid of attempting new challenges. Just watch carefully to make sure he is safe. For example, when he clambers onto a bed or chair, stand close to him and teach him to turn his body and descend feet first. Keep him busy with activities and games he obviously enjoys, and that catch his attention.

Up to 24 months

- ▲ Change his position often. Let him sit on a small chair that supports his back so that he has a good view of his surroundings.
- ▲ At an early stage, place him on a rug on the floor, surrounded by brightly coloured objects, so that he can experience and discover his surroundings from this position.
- ▲ While you change his nappy, let him kick against your hands, and pump his little legs in a playful way.
- ▲ Regularly allow him to lie and kick his legs without a nappy.
- ▲ Carry him in a kangaroo bag or papoose tied around your body while you do your tasks around the house – this teaches him to adjust his balance according to your movements.
- ▲ Place him on the lawn on a blanket – on his tummy, back, and at least for a little while without a nappy (if the weather permits). This is another stimulating environment.
- ▲ Encourage him to reach for objects. This is basic exploring behaviour. When a baby reaches out and grabs an object, encourage him to do it again.
- ▲ Play 'ride the horse' by jogging him on your knee or foot.
- ▲ When he begins to move forward when lying on his tummy, encourage him to start crawling by placing his toys slightly out of his reach.
- ▲ A sit-and-ride tricycle (or anything that he can push or pull) is an excellent toy for developing motor as well as spatial skills and will give your infant endless pleasure.

- Take him to the play park and let him swing and clamber and hang on the apparatus. If the swing has a flat seat, let him lie on his tummy on the seat, and slowly move the swing backwards and forwards.
- Help him to hang by his arms. Hold him while he is hanging. As his arm and shoulder muscles develop, he will begin to hang by himself. Be there when he lets go so that you can catch him.
- Encourage him to climb in and out of car tyres, to crawl over and under, to run forwards and to change direction. Join in his activities and enjoy the way he shouts with laughter at his mother's antics. Teach him vocabulary while you play, and ask him, when he has the necessary vocabulary, to describe what you are doing.
- Hold his hands and jump on a trampoline with him.

THREE TO SIX YEARS

You do not have to make special time for these games and activities but they can form part of your and your child's daily routine. There are many wonderful opportunities, inside and outside the house, that you can use to stimulate your child's movement. Let him play and play and play ...

Encourage your child to move, explore and discover as much as possible.Take him for walks in nature. Go for walks on the beach, in the veld, on the mountain, swimming, playing ball.

These are all activities that encourage physical **movement**, balance and co-ordination, and they also provide an ideal opportunity for interaction between parent and child.

At all times, keep the importance of language development in mind; make use of every possible opportunity to talk to your child and encourage him to talk to you also.

At **bath time**, let your child move towards the bathroom in different ways: crawling, dragging himself along on his tummy, walking on all fours like a monkey, jumping with two feet together, jumping on one leg, hopping like a rabbit or a frog, and waggling like a duck. Older toddlers can do a combination of these movements. Bath time will become fun while, at the same time, your child is practising different motor skills.

Transform **routine instructions** into games; for example 'Hop, jump, crawl to Daddy and tell him to come and drink his tea'.

When you send your child to fetch or put something away, give **silly instructions**; for example 'Jump in the air three times, and hop around the table on one leg, then put your book away, please'. Give a younger toddler two instructions at first, and when he can remember and do this comfortably, give him three instructions. This also promotes listening skills.

You can give similar instructions outdoors; for example, 'Run around the tree and then hand me the garden fork, please'. In the kitchen, 'Clap your hands three times, turn around twice; take the milk out of the fridge, and put it on the table, please'.

Tie one end of a **rope** or string to the washing-line post or to the leg of a chair; slowly move the other end from side to side, just above the ground, and let your toddler jump over it.

Once he has mastered this skill, he will quickly learn to skip with a skipping rope on his own. Encourage this.

Tell your child to **roll** on the carpet or lawn like a log of wood with his arms above his head. Let him roll from side to side and then repeat the movement with his arms at his sides. This game promotes the co-ordination of back, neck, shoulder and hip muscles. (Of course, it is even more fun when Mom or Dad rolls too!)

Throw a **blanket** on the lawn or rug and hold one end. Let your toddler lie on the other end, grasp it and then roll himself into the blanket (towards you), and then roll out again.

Encourage your toddler to roll down **sand dunes** and **grassy banks**. He can also try to roll up a slight incline.

Older toddlers enjoy trying to **walk like a crab**. Let your toddler sit on the floor with his legs bent in front of him, feet flat on the ground. He puts his hands on either side of his body, slightly to the back, lifts his bottom up and walks backwards and forwards, then sideways like a crab.

Again, it is even more fun when Mummy or Daddy join in! Alternate this game with other imitations – let your toddler make his own suggestions and join in the fun.

Teach your toddler to play the whole range of **jumping games** (Hop Scotch and others). Make up your own rules for **Ladder Jumping**: place a ladder flat on the lawn. Let your child jump between the rungs in every possible way: feet together, backwards and forwards, with feet on either side of the ladder, and then inside; on one leg – every way you can think of.

Any child will enjoy this.

Children are crazy about **obstacles**. Work out an obstacle course; for example, crawl under the table, climb over the chair, jump over a rope tied to two chairs, jump on one leg around the table and end up with a somersault on the rug.

1 Climb onto the highest cable spool, step onto the next, jump down.
2 Clamber up and down the rope ladder.
3 Climb to the top of the rope and climb down.
4 Cross the log heel-toe, or jump from side to side with both feet together, or give huge steps from side to side.
5 Balance on the first tyre, and step onto the next, then the next without falling off. If you fall off, start again. Or crawl through the first tyre, change direction and crawl through the next and so on.
6 Jump onto the tube, jump into the tube, jump on the other side and jump down. Or jump across it from side to side with feet together (change the movements to suit your child's age and development, and alternate them to keep the game interesting).
7 Crawl through the blanket tunnel.

You can construct a more permanent obstacle course in the garden. Use old car tyres, tubes, crates or large wooden cable spools at different heights, wooden poles or logs, a rope ladder, ropes, and so on. Car tyres can be planted into the ground in an upright position, or used flat on the ground.

Build your own play paradise

You can use just about anything, costing you very little or next to nothing, to build a playground in the garden for your child. Give your imagination free rein and use whatever you can lay your hands on.

Keep the following in mind when you plan the playground:

- The **space** available.
- **Versatility**: it should be suitable for the various areas of development.
- Using it should present your child with **challenges** without being too difficult.
- It should be **safe**. Make sure no screws or nails are exposed, and that there are no rough edges that can cause injuries.

You can use the following materials:

- Old cable spools of different sizes to vary the height. Place them as illustrated, or on their sides so your child crawl through.
- Make a rope ladder and tie it to a tree stump or make knots in a thick rope and tie it to a thick tree stump so that your child can climb up and down, hang or swing on the rope. The knots will make it easier to grasp and prevent his hands from slipping.
- A longish tree stump with a diameter of about 30 cm can be used as a balancing bar. Let your child walk across heel-toe, or jump from side to side with two feet together.
- Old car tyres. Take the size into account. Your toddler should be able to crawl through the tyre once it has been planted in the ground.
- Halved tyres can be used for climbing over, scrambling from one tyre to another, running between tyres, and so on.
- A tyre can also be tied to a tree trunk with a thick rope to make a swing.
- A large tractor tube, firmly inflated, makes a wonderful trampoline that can be used for various activities.
- Stitch up the sides of an old blanket so that your child can crawl through.
- Use a large empty plastic drum for your child to roll to and fro on his tummy, or to balance on while rolling it forward with his feet.

- Use large coffee tins filled with concrete (or sand) for steps. Paint them in bright colours.

Give your imagination free rein and use whatever is available. Children often prefer playing with everyday articles.

Milestones for development and co-ordination of fine motor muscles

Smaller movements, for example of the hands, fingers, eyes, tongue and toes, require what is known as fine motor skills, which depend on the development of the fine muscles. Babies explore their surroundings mostly with their hands and fingers – they touch objects to determine the texture, shape and size. But all movements are led by a child's eyes, which is why well-developed eye muscles are essential for fine muscle co-ordination.

When you put your finger in a new-born baby's hand, he will grab it – this is a reflex and he has no control over it. But he gradually gains more control over this kind of movement, at the same time learning to focus both eyes on objects. The development of these skills is characterised by the following milestones:

Birth to 10 weeks

At this stage, your baby's hands are usually clenched, and he will grasp your finger or any object you place in his hands with a reflex movement. He will still be learning to focus his eyes. At 8 to 10 weeks he will begin opening his hands.

Three to six months

At three months his hands are usually open so that his fingers can move more voluntarily. He can hold a rattle or toy for a while and begins to reach out for objects. He holds his hands close to his face and studies them with great concentration. At four to five months he begins to touch and grab objects. He plays with his feet if there are no interesting objects within reach. He will also suck his toes.

Six to nine months

He uses his eyes when he reaches for objects and adjusts the position of his hands according to what he sees. At six months he begins to hold his bottle and can switch an object from one hand to the other. He also puts objects into his mouth to explore them further. He will try to grab anything that looks interesting and can hold small objects in his hands, pressing them between palm and fingers. At nine months he can grasp finger food between his thumb and forefinger, even though he cannot always put it in his mouth properly. He can take toys out of a container, or put them back, and hand something to you if you ask for it, but will still struggle a bit to let go.

He can hold an object in each hand. He can point at something, even though he cannot say what he wants. He can also hold a spoon and will try to feed himself, although it will be a rather messy affair! You can begin teaching him to drink milk, juice and water from a special beaker with a lid, a spout and two handles.

Ten to 12 months

Your child is becoming more and more skilled using his fingers and can hold smaller objects between thumb and forefinger. For example, he will pluck fluff from your rugs and furniture with great concentration. At about ten months he lets go of objects, and then the fun begins – he enjoys dropping objects so that Mom or Dad can pick them up. He can bring his hands together and clap his hands.

Thirteen to 18 months

Your child will begin to bend his wrists and to use his hand independently of his arm – at about 15 months most babies can wave good-bye. He begins to combine movements, for example to hold something and to turn it around, or to open and shut something. At 18 months his hand skills are fairly sophisticated. He can build two-piece puzzles, and a tower consisting of three or four blocks. He will scribble if you put a crayon in his hand, and can turn the pages of a cardboard book. He can take off his shoes, and pull up a zipper if you show him how to do it.

Twenty to 24 months

He can control objects that are further away from his hand, for example a toy on a rope. He can screw a lid onto a container, or unscrew it, and turn a door knob. Washing his hands is great fun, and he will enjoy rolling the soap in his hands to make foam. He now begins using predominantly the right or the left hand, but at this stage one cannot determine whether he is going to be right or left handed. He uses his thumb, index finger and middle finger, and develops a better grasp of a pencil or crayon. He will attempt to trace vertical lines, as well as a circle if you show him how. He can put his shoes on, usually the wrong shoe on the wrong foot, but cannot fasten them yet. He does not mess as much when he eats, and can remove sweets from their wrappers himself. His towers consist of several blocks.

Two to three years

Your toddler will start using crayons more single-mindedly (not only to scribble). He will try to dress and undress himself, and to button up his clothing. Encourage him and allow him to try. He will build towers with more attention to detail (eight to ten blocks), and can build a bridge with three blocks if you show him how to do it. He can also use his thumb separately from his other fingers.

Three to four years

He begins to draw recognisable pictures and as his eye-hand co-ordination improves, also lines, circles, a V-shape, and perhaps trace a T-shape and a cross. He will be quite skillful at using a pair of blunt-ended scissors.

Four to five years

Your child can use his fingers separately, and hold a pencil between his thumb, index finger and middle finger. His people figures have a head, body and limbs; he can draw inside diagonal and straight lines; and he can draw basic shapes (circle, square, triangle).

Towers and construction become more complex. He can also cut along a straight line. He is better at dressing and undressing himself, but is still unable to cope with small buttons. He can open and shut taps to wash his hands. He uses both hands to put toothpaste on his toothbrush.

Five to six years

He can thread shoe laces through the holes according to a pattern, and tie them. His drawings of people contain greater detail and he can colour in pictures. He cuts accurately and can do simple embroidery with wool and a thick needle. At the age of six he knows which is his right hand and he can write letters, figures and short words, *without necessarily knowing what he is writing.*

LEFT- OR RIGHT-HANDED?

Your child has no control over which hand is dominant – this is determined by his brain, as one of the two sides become dominant as the brain develops. There is no proof that it is better to be left- or right-handed, or that one hand can execute certain tasks better than the other hand. If your child's brain determines that he is left-handed, you will be doing him an injustice by forcing him to change this. It could lead to confusion and a great deal of frustration.

Games and activities for fine motor co-ordination

Encourage each stage of your baby's development from the very first day. Choose games and activities according to your child's level of development. Encourage him from the beginning to reach out for objects by hanging a colourful **mobile** above his bed. Or hold a colourful toy, preferably one that makes **sounds**, and move it so that he can follow it with his eyes. Let him touch objects with different textures and give him a rattle he can hold and shake.

Surround him with **balls** in different sizes, and large **construction toys** such as blocks or empty cartons. The blocks are first for looking at and touching, and later to build towers. Use larger blocks for younger toddlers, and smaller blocks for older toddlers. Any construction toys, such as Duplo™, Lego™, Lasy™ and Stickle Bricks™, provide good exercise.

Plastic bottles in different sizes with screw-on lids can keep your toddlers happy for hours and exercise his fingers. Give him thick **crayons** and an old exercise book or magazine for scribbling in, and a thick brush and non-toxic paint. Water-based poster paint in an empty roll-on deodorant bottle works well. Finger paint is always popular and can be used by very young children (*see* page 119 for recipe).

A simple **shape sorter** can keep your infant busy from an early age, even if initially he merely examines the coloured plastic shapes and only uses them 'correctly' at a later stage.

Make sure your infant has enough **cardboard books** to page through, and talk to him about the pictures and the story. Let him point out specific objects, and allow him to turn the pages himself. The pictures in the book must contain few details, and have simple lines and bright colours.

Hints for buying crayons, paint and scissors

- Wax crayons are available in different thicknesses, to fit your toddler's grip. Use short, thick wax crayons for toddlers between one and two years. Older toddlers can use thinner crayons.
- Buy some powder paint. The three basic colours are sufficient. Mix the paint with cooked starch (Maizena porridge) to a creamy thickness. This mixture is less messy than ordinary runny paint, and can also be used as finger paint. Toddlers prefer broad brushes with long handles. Collect old calendars and let children paint on the back of the printed pages – display their artwork in the kitchen and in their nursery.
- Buy a pair of blunt-ended scissors. Plastic scissors are available, but toddlers acquire cutting skills sooner with a good pair of blunt-ended steel scissors. Blunt scissors are difficult to cut with and may discourage your child from learning to cut. Cutting exercises the thumb and index finger which is essential for good pencil control.

As soon as he wants to put his shoes on, or take them off himself, show him **which shoe** goes on **which foot**, and say 'This is your right shoe; it goes on your right foot'. Make a song about it and make sure it remains a game without putting pressure on him to remember right and left. That will automatically come later.

Threading activities are always popular and very good exercise for eye-hand co-ordination. Press small holes in a cardboard shape, give him thick string or ribbon, with the points finished off with a piece of cellotape so that he can push them through the holes easily. Make cardboard shoe shapes with holes on the right places for threading laces through. Use string in two colours, so that you can teach him to **tie the laces**, and eventually to make a bow. Older toddlers will enjoy threading beads, but need to be watched carefully so that they do not swallow the beads or put them in their ears or nostrils.

FINGER GAMES

Finger games are also good. There are many finger rhymes. These strengthen the fingers and exercise your child's concentration and memory, and extend his vocabulary:

Tommy Thumb, Tommy Thumb,	*toddler hides hands behind*
where are you?	*his back*
Here I am! Here I am!	*first shows one thumb, wiggles it,*
And how do you do?	*then the other, wiggles*
	hands behind back

Do the same with Peter Pointer (index finger), Long Man (middle finger), Ring Man (ring finger), Pinkie.

Fingers, Fingers, where are you?	*hands behind back*
Here we are! Here we are!	*shows hands and wriggles fingers*
And how do you do?	*clap hands*

This little piggy went to market	*shows thumb*
This little piggy stayed at home	*shows index finger*
This little piggy had roast beef	*shows middle finger*
This little piggy had none, and	*shows ring finger*
This little piggy went "Wee, wee,	*shows pinkie and wiggles it*
wee all the way home!"	

Repeat the rhyme so that both hands can be used alternately, and eventually both hands together

Let your toddler recite the names of his fingers, Tommy Thumb, Peter Pointer, Long Man, Ring Man, Pinkie, first wiggling his thumb, then putting each finger against his thumb as it is named. This is repeated backwards, starting with the little finger, then with his other hand. This game strengthens his fingers, and improves concentration.

Let your child play imitation games with his hands and fingers: stars that twinkle or electric lights that go on and off – he makes a fist and shoots his fingers forward.

Use what you have

Give your child scissors and a pile of old **magazines** and let him cut out to his heart's content. He can paste his own artwork with the pictures he cut out. Cut and paste activities are invaluable for the development of eye-hand co-ordination. You can also draw simple shapes, which your child can fill in with mosaic patterns by tearing and pasting magazine pictures.

What child can resist **crumpling** and tearing paper? Let your child make a game of crumpling or tearing up all the daily junk mail and to throw it in the dust bin. We all receive lots of junk mail. First let him use his hands to crumple the pages into a small ball. Then he can stand away from the dust bin and see how accurately he can throw the balls into the dust bin. When his hands are stronger, he can alternate using the left and the right hand.

Plasticine and play dough provide a lot of fun. Let your child roll balls and snakes and press out patterns (*see* recipe on page 20). Give your child a corner in the garden where he can make mudpies to his heart's content.

A container with **coins**, **shells**, **beads**, **matches** and **buttons** to sort and put into separate containers can occupy your toddler in a positive way. It improves his eye-hand co-ordination, and teaches him to concentrate.

Older toddlers can be given a pair of tweezers for this game – it is more difficult to pick objects up with tweezers than with the fingers, and is an excellent exercise for fine muscle co-ordination.

To make the game even more interesting, let him pick up beads between his knuckles and put them in a container.

Tie loose **knots** in **thick string** and ask your child to undo the knots. Use thinner string for older toddlers.

Let your child hammer **nails** into a piece of wood. Toddlers are crazy about woodwork. Pieces of leftover wood, rags, corks, polystyrene, icecream sticks, and so on are all fun to play with. The hammer must not be too heavy or big for your toddler to handle. Use nails in medium and thick sizes so that he can comfortably hold them between thumb and index finger. Avoid dirty or rusted nails, which may cause infection if your child injures himself with them. At some stage or another he will hit a finger, but

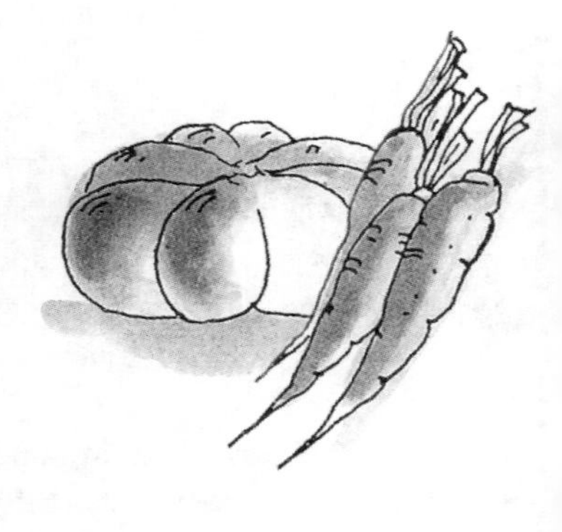

this is not sufficient reason to discourage this activity. Be there and ready to comfort him if it does happen.

Special woodwork sets are available for toddlers.

Washing pegs race: let your child see how quickly he can peg ten pegs onto a towel and remove them again. Add more and more pegs, or give him time to peg them right around the towel.

Card games improve concentration and exercise several other skills. There are various kinds of children's cards on the market, with pictures, shapes, figures, with opposites and similarities the child can sort, and cards for memory games or 'Snap'. Ordinary playing cards (hearts, clover, diamonds, and so on) are also suitable. Card games improve eye-hand co-ordination, concentration, short-term memory, visual discrimination and number concepts.

Older toddlers will enjoy **folding** hats, boats and airplanes from **paper** – and then trying them out – can the boat float in water (keep a large container of water ready), and can the airplane fly?

Balance

When your infant starts walking, he holds his feet far apart and his hands in the air to keep his balance. As this skill improves, he brings his feet closer together and drops his arms. Before long he can squat or bend down to lift something without toppling over. His balance improves a lot between two and three years as his centre of gravity shifts and he can see and focus better.

As he learns to balance better, he also becomes aware of the two sides of his body – a left side and a right side. Good balance is essential for good posture and to prevent your child from becoming tired too soon. Good eye-foot co-ordination also contributes to good balance.

Games and activities for balance

Your child can participate in games and activities for balance at a young age.

- When you go for a walk, let him walk on the **kerb** of the pavement, or on a rope on the ground, while holding his hand. His confidence will grow and he will overcome possible fear of heights by walking on a low wall while you hold his hand.
- Make **stilts** with two empty jam tins. Make two holes for thin rope to pass through in the sides at the bottom of each tin. For each stilt, cut a piece of rope long enough for both ends to touch the ground if your toddler holds it in his hand. Tie a knot at one end of the rope (big enough to ensure that the rope will not be pulled through the hole) and thread it from the inside of the tin through one hole and from the outside through the other hole. Tie a knot at the other end of the rope. The rope must form a long loop. Your toddler pulls this tight and holds it in his hands when he walks on the stilts.

- Let your toddler pick up a pencil with his **toes** and pass it to a friend. This not only improves balance, but also concentration and co-ordination.
- Let your child **jump on one leg** whenever the opportunity arises– incorporate this into routine tasks during the day, for example at bath time (*see* page 58). Alternate this with walking tip-toe, backwards and forwards, jumping with feet together, and so on.
- Let him walk on a low wall or on a wooden beam when the opportunity arises. Let him walk step by step with the right heel touching the left toe before shifting the left foot and the left heel touching the right toe – in this way he can feel that he is **balancing**.
- Let him walk in your **footprints** on the beach.
- Make him his own **balancing board** with a plank over a piece of pipe or a stone. While balancing on the balancing board, he can do tricks, for example bouncing a ball or touching different parts of his body. But remember, it must remain a game and not begin to feel like being coached, otherwise the activity loses its element of play.
- Play **statues**. Your child moves around and as soon as you clap your hands he must stop and stand like a statue in the position he finds himself. Count to see how long he can stand still in the same position.
- Play **knee soccer**. Both you and your child kneel down (outside on the lawn or on a carpet inside the house). You 'kick' the ball towards the child using your knee, and he must stop the ball with his legs or arms. Once he has stopped the ball, he must kick it to you using his knee. If he does not stop the ball, you win a goal. If he can kick it past you, he scores a goal. This game is fun on the beach as well.
- Any **kick-the-ball game** develops balancing skills. Stuff a strong plastic bag full of crumpled paper (let your toddler help you), tie it up and tie another bag around it to make it very strong. This makes a good ball to kick around and to throw; your toddler will have control over it because it cannot roll away, and it won't break windows. And when it is worn, you simply make another one.
- **Target kicking**: Place empty plastic bottles filled with sand in a row, a metre or two apart. Let your child dribble his home-made ball between the bottles, alternating his feet. Place the bottles closer to one another as your child's skill improves.

Signs of problems with muscle development and co-ordination

If your child shows any signs that his gross or fine muscle development and co-ordination are not on target, take him to an occupational therapist as soon as possible so that the problem can be diagnosed and addressed. Use the milestones discussed earlier as a guideline. The following may also be signs of problems:

- **Clumsiness**: a clumsy child falls frequently or bumps against objects.
- **Poor self-image**: Because your child does not have normal muscle co-ordination he is less daring and does not enjoy experimenting. At the age of four or five, a child will become aware that he cannot keep up with other children and this will damage his self-image.
- **Lack of concentration**: A child lacking postural endurance will find it more difficult to concentrate because he will become tired very quickly.
- **Poor posture**: The most comfortable position for a child with a lack of postural endurance is to lie down because he tires easily. He will prefer to play lying down rather than sitting up.

When clumsiness is a problem

Initially all babies are clumsy when they are learning to walk – they walk with legs apart, arms held high in the air to balance, but they fall frequently, and still bump against chairs and other objects because they do not have control over this activity.

With practice they develop the necessary muscle co-ordination and for most children the general clumsiness is a thing of the past soon enough . By the time they go to school, they can hop, run, and do somersaults and cartwheels. A handful of children do not shake off this basic clumsiness before they go to school. This can be ascribed to poor muscle co-ordination. A clumsy child often feels inferior and is also teased by other children. Clumsiness is something that cannot be concealed, and if your child remains considerably clumsy (*see* Signs of problems on page 73), you should take him to an occupational therapist for diagnosis and treatment.

SIGNS OF PROBLEMS

These signs of problems should be placed within the context of your toddler's age. A mother's intuition would usually tell her that her child's progress is too slow or that he has problems. Get professional help immediately if your toddler shows any of these signs:

- falls too frequently;
- cannot get up when he is lying on his back;
- cannot jump over something without holding onto something or somebody;
- cannot throw or catch a ball and handles it clumsily;
- cannot hit a ball with a bat or club;
- avoids certain physical activities, for example playing on jungle gym with friends;
- cannot hop, skip or jump;
- cannot ride a bicycle without help;
- battles to learn to swim;
- is excessively afraid of heights;
- holds his pen awkwardly;
- cannot hit a nail into a piece of wood.

Body image

Body image is a child's subjective experience of his body and its possibilities. A small child's discovery of his own body as 'me' is a special milestone in his development.

Through observation, your baby realises that he is himself. At about four months a baby begins to distinguish between himself and his mother. Before this age he is not aware of himself as a separate person and he cannot distinguish between what is 'me' and what is 'not me'. Gradually he begins to discover his own body and learns to distinguish certain parts of his body as his own – his hands, fingers, feet and toes.

Your baby also gradually learns that when he uses his body he can manipulate his environment. When he throws down a toy, you pick it up; when he knocks together two objects, they make a noise. He examines objects with his mouth and becomes aware that he can carry out certain actions with separate objects.

Play with and talk to your child so that he learns about his own body. While bathing and dressing him, or changing his nappy, talk to him and make constant comments about what you are doing, for example, 'Mummy is washing your face, then your body, first one arm and then the hand, another arm and another hand', and so on. Teach him, for example, to bash two objects together by holding his hands and executing the movement with him. In this way he becomes aware that he is using his body to carry out the actions; the sounds will develop his listening skills and the movements will develop his muscles.

Your child's self-image flows from his body image. A child who develops a healthy body image, in other words, who gains self-knowledge by broadening his field of experience, testing his own abilities and developing a sense of independence, will have more self-confidence to explore and discover further.

A good body image and a good self-image are very important for school-readiness.

Awareness of body

This is the ability to distinguish between the different parts of the body. A child must have an innate awareness of his body and the position of the different parts of his body. He must be able to distinguish between all the parts of his body and know what they can do. Therefore, awareness of the body implies the following:

- Knowing the different parts of the body: these are my arms, legs, etc.
- Knowing what the different parts of the body can do: I clap my hands, stamp my feet, nod my head, swing my arms from side to side, etc.
- Knowing how to move the different parts of the body effectively.

Laterality

Laterality is an awareness of the fact that the body has two sides, a left side and a right side, and that there are similarities and differences between the two sides: I have an arm and a hand on both sides of my body but can do things better with my right hand, for example. Your child gradually learns that each side of his body has a name, right side and left side. From about three and a half years he is aware of the difference, even if he cannot name the sides correctly before the age of six. Dominance and awareness of direction develop from laterality. Both are is essential for learning reading, writing and maths skills.

Awareness of direction also depends on a process of maturing, as well as on experience. Once your child can determine the position of objects to the left or right of himself, he will also be able to identify movement to the right or to the left, and will be able to move in a direction as instructed.

Games and activities for laterality

Any games with instructions containing the words 'left' or 'right' are suitable. In the beginning you can use **colour coding** for 'left' and 'right'.

Stick red and green circles on the wall, for example two red and one green circle. Repeat the pattern a few times. The child must press his right hand on the red circles and his left hand on the green circles. Initially, tie a red band around his right wrist and a green band around his left wrist to make it easier for him.

Give instructions such as, 'Move (walk, hop, jump) two steps to the right, and one step to the left, three steps to the right, and two steps to the left'. At first, stand in front of your child and point to his right and left.

When your child is more familiar with 'left' and 'right' you can give instructions such as 'Touch your left foot with your right hand', or 'Touch your right eye with your left hand'.

Paste a large sheet of paper on a smooth wall. Draw a figure eight horizontally on the paper and let your child trace it with wax crayons: from right to left with the crayon in his right hand, and from left to right with the crayon in his left hand.

6

Development of the mind

Your child's genes determine her potential in any area. But whether this potential will be fully realised depends on the stimulation a child receives. From the beginning, a baby's intellectual and emotional development progresses at the same pace as her physical development. You can see and note how she grows and becomes heavier, how her use of her muscles and co-ordination improve, and that she can see and hear better.

The development of intellectual skills, which eventually enable her to think, reason, talk and remember, are not as clearly visible from the beginning. But these skills are developing from the word go, which is why it is so important that you provide an environment at an early stage that will stimulate and encourage her intellectual development.

Learning is fun

From day one your baby is the most enthusiastic and receptive pupil you could ever have. Her brain is like a sponge that absorbs every piece of information made available. She wants to examine, to know, to learn, and she wants to please you.

This combination is what makes her such a wonderful pupil – exploit it and make the most of every moment. Expose her to new experiences, give her new things to explore, play games that help her discover what she is capable of, what the world around her looks like, and how it functions. Talk to her even before birth, and continue talking after her birth.

Show her pictures, read her stories and give her detailed descriptions of what the things around her look like and what is happening. Play with her and encourage her with praise and support. If your child enjoys learning, she will never want to stop learning.

Do not expect anything from her that is beyond her ability – that will frustrate her and hamper her natural urge to discover things.

Give her opportunities and guidance, but do not force her into anything. When she is ready to move from one milestone to another, she will do it naturally – and derive great pleasure from what she achieves, and in each new skill she masters.

An older child who simply cannot remember the dates of historical events when writing a history test is often able to recite all the names and home provinces of the new cricket team without hesitation. This is because she finds history boring, but may be intensely interested in cricket.

For the same reason, you can help your child towards school-readiness far better by playing card games that teach her the names of cars, or by singing her the words of her favourite songs rather than by teaching her the alphabet in isolation.

Language development

My previous book, *Clever Talk* (Metz Press 1999), is about language development and how absolutely simple it is to give your child a real advantage in life by helping her develop her language and listening skills. Do try to obtain a copy if you do not already have it.

This chapter is largely based on the book.

Language development is the basis of intellectual development. Your child's language ability determines to what extent she will realise her intellectual potential.

It affects her interaction with everyone around her, her self-image, eagerness to learn, her social and emotional development, her concept of moral values, and her ability to distinguish between right and wrong.

It is almost as essential for your child to learn to talk as it is to breathe – her survival as a person in her own right depends on her language ability, because everything she learns will revolve around language.

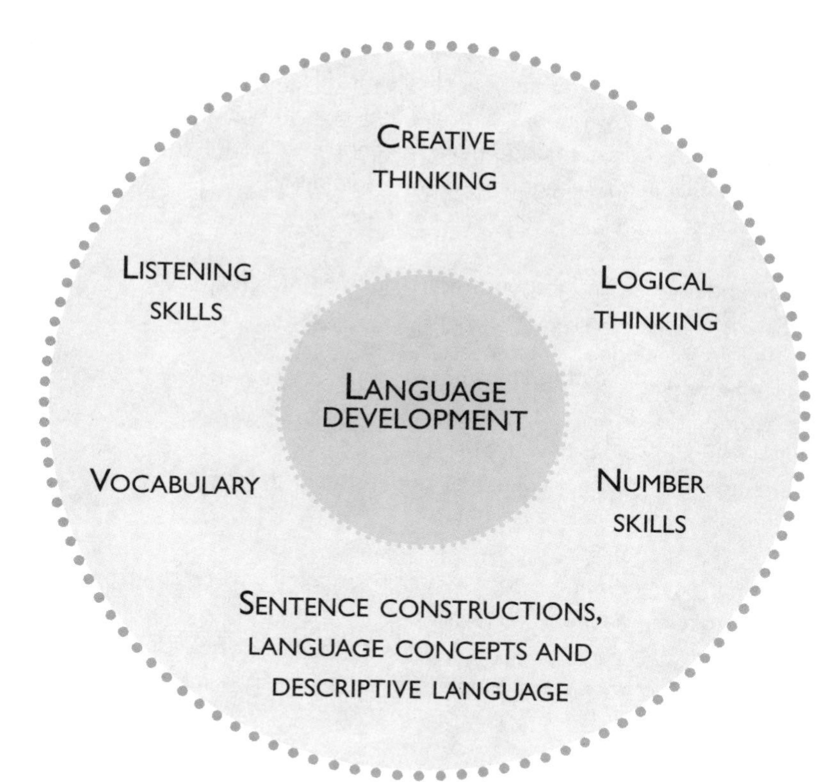

Auditory perception

Just as language development is essential for your child's intellectual development, satisfactory development of auditory perception is crucial to language development. This was fully discussed on pages 44 to 46. Read it again, and bear this in mind when you look at the milestones for language development.

Milestones for language development

From the beginning, two processes are involved in language development: what your infant hears and understands, and what she says. As far as the use of language as such is concerned, we talk about her receptive vocabulary (what she understands) on one hand, and her expressive vocabulary (what she says) on the other hand.

A new-born baby first communicates by different ways of crying, then with the first smile, then gurgling, which becomes babbling with voice intonations.

At the age of about 15 months, most infants say their first real words. This develops rapidly and by 18 months your child should have a vocabulary of about 50 words, say her own name, and use sentences of about two words. From the age of two years, language development progresses at an unbelievable pace, and your infant's vocabulary grows enormously.

Two years

- ▲ She understands and responds when given instructions.
- ▲ She knows the words for obvious parts of the body.
- ▲ She likes listening to stories.
- ▲ Her expressive vocabulary consists of 200 to 400 words.
- ▲ She understands about 1 000 words.
- ▲ She uses three-word sentences.
- ▲ She understands simple questions and responds to them.

Two and a half years

- ▲ She can say her name.
- ▲ She begins to use the correct word order.
- ▲ She listens attentively to a story, but cannot relate it afterwards.
- ▲ She begins to understand simple adjectives and uses words such as big and small.

Three years

- ▲ She can say her name and surname.
- ▲ Her expressive vocabulary consists of about 450 words.
- ▲ She can say how old she is and that she is a girl.
- ▲ She understands longer and more complicated sentences.
- ▲ She can repeat three figures.
- ▲ She can respond to an instruction with three parts, for example, 'Take your teddy and put it away in your room'.
- ▲ She can tell you about some event that occurred.
- ▲ About 80 per cent of her spoken language is understandable.

Three and a half years

- ▲ She can tell how many brothers and sisters she has.
- ▲ She enjoys talking to herself.

- She finds it easier to listen.
- She can repeat three to four figures.
- She indicates future in her sentences, for example, 'Later I'm going for a walk with Mummy'.
- She sings along and remembers parts of songs.

Four years

- She makes few grammatical errors.
- She asks endless questions and likes to use words such as 'why?'.
- She understands and uses words such as 'who, when, and what'.
- Her expressive vocabulary consists of about 1 000 words.

Four and a half years

- She pronounces almost all her words correctly.
- She can repeat four figures.
- Her expressive vocabulary consists of about 1 500 words.
- She uses the comparative and superlative degrees, for example bigger and biggest.
- She can respond to instructions involving something she cannot see when she receives the instruction, for example, 'Please go and fetch my soft scarf on the bed in my bedroom'.

Five years

- She can hold a proper conversation.
- Her sentences become more complicated.
- She uses different kinds of sentences, for example questions, commands, negatives, etc.
- She asks relevant questions and can answer them.
- She uses conjunctions such as 'but', 'because', 'if'.
- She can form nouns from related verbs, for example 'paint, painter', 'build, builder'.
- Her expressive vocabulary consists of about 2 200 words.
- She uses most personal pronouns and possessives (I, me, mine, you, yours, he, she, them) correctly.
- She can say the day and month of her birthday.
- She can repeat four to five figures.
- She uses the past tense correctly.
- She knows easy opposites (little and lots, hard and soft).

Six years

- She knows all the days of the week.
- She uses 'yesterday', 'today' and 'tomorrow' correctly.
- She can repeat five figures and count up to ten objects.
- Her expressive vocabulary consists of about 3 000 words.
- She understands and uses words such as 'on top', 'behind', 'in front', 'near' and 'between'.
- She understands verbal problems and can respond to them and give answers.
- She understands and describes similarities and differences between objects.
- She can identify the coins in our monetary system and knows what is worth the most.

Games and activities for language development

Teach your child from the beginning to listen accurately and to interpret what she hears. This is an important skill a child must develop for learning language and building a vocabulary.

In fact, listening skills are not only essential for learning a language, but for all learning.

Listening skills

There are a great many games you can play with your child to develop her listening skills. Always remember, however, that learning should be fun and that it should never be too difficult. Success builds self-confidence. Never allow your child to feel that she is stupid or that she has failed. These games can be played in the course of the day, when the opportunity arises, at home, in the garden or in the car. Always keep them natural and spontaneous.

Various listening skills kan be practised with specific games:

Differentiate between different sounds (Auditory discrimination)

Make your child aware, from a young age, of different **sounds** in and around the house. For example, your baby will soon learn to point to the microwave when it goes 'ping', or to the front door when the doorbell rings. Imitate the sounds and point out specific sounds, for example when you run the bathwater, when the water drains away, the sound of an electric beater, a kettle boiling, the washing machine, the sound of her father's car and the dog barking, and so on.

Help her to understand, through games, the concept of sounds that are **high** and **low**, **loud** and **soft**, **far away** and **close by**, **slow** and **fast**.

For example, tell her to squat down when you speak in a low voice, or to stretch her arms high up in the air when you speak in a high voice.

Do the same with loud, soft, fast and slow. For example, she can fold her arms when you speak softly, clap her hands when you speak loudly, or run short steps when you speak fast, and take long, slow strides when you speak slowly. Children love such games.

Hand-clapping games can be played at an early age. Say a few names with your child's name in between, and let her clap her hands when she hears her name, for example, 'Mary, Tommy, Susie (clap), Freddy, Carla, Susie (clap)'. Play along with her, hold her hands and clap each time you say her name. Eventually you can say the names quite rapidly and she will soon know when to clap.

The next game could be "Clap your hands every time you hear an 's'". Then say different sounds, with an 's' once or twice in-between.

Say some sounds louder than others, so that she must listen carefully to hear the clapping sound. In this way you will make her conscious of sounds at an early age.

Play '**I spy with my little eye**'. This is a wonderful game because you can adjust it according to what you want your child to learn. It works well for sound differentiation and children enjoy it from an early age. Say, 'I spy with my little eye something that begins with a 't'!'

Vary the game by using different sounds. Once your toddler becomes more familiar with the sounds and she guesses correctly, give her a turn to try to catch you out.

Association

Ask an older toddler who already has an extensive vocabulary to associate words she hears and the objects the words describe. Toddlers between five and six like **lists** – they will enjoy these games.

Use these examples or make up your own lists about things you know your toddler likes:

For example, ask, 'What is not food: meat, flowers, pumpkin?' or 'What is not fruit: orange, fish, apple, peach?' and so on.

Or let her give words that fit a specific object or can be associated with it, for example bird: feathers, beak, claws, wings, nest, eggs; or fish, sea, fins, scales, bait, fishing net, fishing rod.

Or ask, 'Who does what?'

Again, give one example and let her complete the other sentences: 'A bird flies; a fish ...; a horse ..., an airplane ...'

Comprehension

Your child should be able to understand correctly what she hears. If you begin talking sense to her from the beginning, she will quickly understand what you are saying.

Most toddlers enjoy this comprehension game because of its silly element.

Who can do what: Ask her 'Can fish swim? Can cats bark? Can we eat bricks? Can dogs climb trees?'

If her vocabulary is well developed, you can ask her to say what is correct when she answers 'No', for example, 'Can we eat bricks?' Her answer could be, 'No, we can eat bread' or 'No, we build with bricks'.

Silly questions: Give your child small tasks, and when you ask for something that is impossible to do, she must say, 'Silly question!', for example:

Bring me the book.
Bring me the floor.
Dress the chair.
Put the blocks away.

It's silly: Your child must recognise and correct tomfoolery. For example, say 'I see with my ears' or 'My hand has three toes' or 'When I swim, I'm dry' and so on. She must correct you.

You could make a story of it; for example, 'The sun comes up at night, then it's dark, and when I close my eyes, I can read my book'. Between her fits of laughter, let her find the suitable words and correct the sentences.

Guess what I'm thinking about? This is one of the most popular and useful games for developing comprehension skills in toddlers. Use pictures and give further clues with words. Your toddler must listen very carefully for clues and guess what you are thinking, for example, 'I'm thinking about something that lives in a tree, has a long tail and likes bananas. Guess what I'm thinking about?' or 'I'm thinking about something with feathers, that waggles when he walks, likes swimming and lives on a farm. Guess what I'm thinking about?' Leave the pictures out to make it slightly more difficult, especially for older toddlers. Say only 'Guess what I'm thinking about. It's in the kitchen, it's round, it has a face, and it makes a tick-tick sound' (wall clock). Give her more clues if she cannot find the answer immediately.

Remembering what she hears (auditory memory)

Your child must develop an ability to retain what she hears, and to recall this information at a later stage. This requires concentration. The best place to begin is with rhymes. Rhymes with sounds that are formed in different places in the mouth exercise the uvula (small tongue), tongue and lips simultaneously, and help her to master difficult sounds, for example:

Lucky Ducky played in muck,
Lucky Ducky got quite stuck.
He made for the bank
Before he sank,
Plucky, Mucky, Lucky Ducky.

(*Nonsense Animal Rhymes*, Kaye Umansky and Chris Fisher, OUP, 2001)

Along the grapevine: This game begins with a statement, and then something is added to it each time. You and your toddler can play it alone, or when she has friends over everybody can play. For example, you begin by saying, 'I'm going to the shop'. Let your toddler repeat what you said and add something new, 'I'm going to the shop to buy an orange'. Now one friend can join in and say, 'I'm going to the shop to buy an orange and a banana', and so on. The first sentence must not be too long. Begin with easier examples and gradually use more difficult sentences as your child's vocabulary grows.

Repeat with me: Give your child short lists of related words that she must then repeat in the same order, for example 'Eye, nose, chin'. Begin with three words, then four, then five, and so on. Do the same with unrelated words, for example, 'Boy, ball, dog'. You can extend this to four, five, or more words. (Just make sure you remember the words in the right order yourself. Your toddler will love catching you out!)

Silly jobs: Give your child simple tasks, with three or four things to do first, for example, 'Jump in the air once, touch your toe, clap your hands three times, and put your tackies away'. This will make putting tackies away a lot more interesting.

Rhymes and songs: Teach your child every rhyme and song you can remember. They never get enough of this.

This will foster a love for song and music and teach her to listen and sing along. Rhymes and songs with actions are always popular – and remember, the more senses that are involved in the process, the better your child will learn.

Breaking words into sounds: Your child must develop the ability to break up words she hears into sounds, for example 'bottom' into 'bot-tom' and 'Mommy' into 'Mom-my'. You can prepare her for this with another clapping game:

Tell her to repeat after you. Clap your hands twice, and tell her to clap twice. When you clap three times, she must also clap three times, and so on. Then add another activity. Clap twice, and give two steps; clap three times, and give three steps.

You can play these games in the venings at bathtime. It will take a bit longer to get to the bathroom, but there are so many other advantages.

Later, add words to the activity. For example, say 'We clap once for every sound in the word. Clap with me, then we give one step for each clap. Dad-dy (two claps and two steps), Mom-my, Ma-ry-Sue, and so on.

Then use bathroom words, such as bath-room, wa-ter, ba-sin, toi-let, with corresponding claps until you are in the bathroom. Your child will enjoy this game from a young age.

Stories and reading

Children acquire language in two ways in particular: when they are spoken to, and when they are read to.

A child's first acquaintance with stories and books is through her parents, and it is never too early to begin. Foster a love and appreciation for stories and books as a source of knowledge and pleasure in your child from a young age. She will become naturally eager to learn to read. Books play a defining role in the four main areas of development.

Books are her first introduction to characters and events outside her world of experience. In children's books this world should be simple and uncomplicated.

Books are her first introduction to 'the arts'. A child who regularly looks at pictures and illustrations systematically develops an appreciation for lines, patterns, textures, as well as the way illustrations depict the story. This is the beginning of visual literacy.

Books promote language development – your child's vocabulary grows and she learns new sound patterns.

Books help your child to give the first steps toward literacy. She learns that the written symbols represent words. She also learns that the symbols are read from left to right, and from the top to the bottom of the page.

A child who is often read to develops a rich verbal language. Stories encourage knowledge of people and worlds she would never experience directly at her age. By the time she goes to school, she will know all about books. To put it simply, she will have a huge advantage.

Social interaction

To tell stories is to share – it brings the teller and the listener together. Story time gives your child an opportunity to experience a combination of language and emotion – communication in its richest form. Therefore, make sure that your child is introduced to books and stories, and the pleasure these bring, from an early age.

Always keep in mind that your child's most important experience should be of enjoyment. She must enjoy sharing the story and pictures, as well as the togetherness and the special bond between you while you are reading and she is listening.

Surround your baby with pictures and books suitable for her age from the very beginning. Strong cardboard books with clear, simple pictures of everyday objects are a good choice as first books.

Page through the books and talk to her about the pictures. Name each object for her. Later, you can ask her, 'Where's the puppy?' 'Where's the cat?' or whatever the pictures are.

Before long she will identify the correct pictures, even before she can say the words. Reading together is a wonderful way to ensure that your child becomes part of the world around her. Our world is making ever-increasing literacy demands on us.

The togetherness with your child while you are reading stories is invaluable. It makes her feel special. It is her time with Mommy or Daddy.

It creates a feeling of security, builds self-confidence, and is a time to enjoy and laugh together. Children enjoy humorous stories and learn a lot from them.

The advantages of reading

To foster a love of reading in your child is invaluable. Not only does it help her to learn to read more easily, it also creates endless educational and learning opportunities you can both enjoy. Make it an enjoyable experience for your child in which she discovers new worlds, and not a painful learning process to which you subject her just because you want an intelligent child. What are the specific advantages to your child when you read to her or tell her stories?

- It stimulates her language development.
- It improves her ability to concentrate.
- It teaches her to listen with attention (she develops listening skills).
- It develops her vocabulary and comprehension skills.
- It broadens her world of experience.
- It stimulates her imagination.
- It teaches her to think in the abstract.
- It helps her gradually to develop an ability to use symbols.
- It helps her understand causes, motives and reasons, and to foresee consequences.
- It gives her an opportunity to hold conversations.
- It teaches her to make choices.
- It helps her build self-confidence.
- It gives her the pleasure of sharing laughter and enjoyment with you.
- It gradually teaches her to read.

Choosing books and stories

You should be very selective with your choice of books for your baby. They should be simple, but contain brightly coloured illustrations. At an early age a baby can follow your finger as you read from a book. Books should be easy to handle and not be easily torn. Hard cardboard and plastic books are ideal choices. Books that make sounds and flaps with hidden illustrations fascinate infants and are ideal to keep them interested, develop listening skills and encourage speech.

Do not force your infant to listen to stories. She will soon let you know what she likes and dislikes.

First read very short stories, but read them regularly. Stories with a strong element of repetition work well. Remember that young children have a very short attention span.

Infants enjoy books with pictures depicting funny scenes, and this can be used to encourage a sense of humour. From the age of one, children begin to see a connection between things they see in books and their environment. For this reason, books that depict everyday scenes, for example a baby bathing, rooms in a house, going shopping, playing in the park, and so on are particularly suitable.

Young children like to be in the story themselves. Substitute the name of the character in the book with your child's name, especially if it is a story with an everyday scene or activities with which she can identify. Always bear in mind that children understand many more words than they can say. They also enjoy trying to pronounce more difficult words.

Very young children enjoy paging through books themselves. Give them enough opportunity to page through a book and look at the pictures, and to ask questions, in that way getting to know the world of the book. Your toddler may at times want to hear the same story over and over. Read it to her every time she asks, even when the story bores you to tears.

Gradually move away from books with everyday themes to less well-known fields to broaden your child's world of experience.

A book with pictures is still important, but older toddlers (between four and six years) need to listen to stories with more text and detail. Most toddlers of this age also enjoy fairy tales.

There are lovely alphabet books available. Page through such books with your toddler, point to each letter and pronounce the sound, not the name of the letter, and then over-emphasise this specific sound in a word, for example 's' (not 'es') for 'sssnake', 'a' for 'apple', 'd' for 'ddaddy', 'r' for 'rrred', 'm' for 'Mmommy', and so on.

Let your toddler name more words with the same sounds. This makes her aware of sounds and helps her to distinguish between different sounds – an important listening skill when she begins to read formally.

There are also books that describe animal activities and encourage the child to mimic, for example, 'Jump like a frog', 'Stand on one leg like a stork', 'Waggle like a duck' and 'Slither like a snake'. Younger children love this, and imitating the physical activity strengthens their verbal understanding of new words and concepts.

INVOLVE YOUR CHILD

Allow your child to choose her own books from time to time. This teaches her to make choices. Ask her why she has chosen a specific book. Allow her to make a particular choice even if you know that the book is beyond her level of development. But ask her to explain why that book is special to her.

Perhaps the cover attracted her. Talk to her about the story if, perhaps, it was not as good as she thought it would be.

Explain to her that, in future, such disappointments may be avoided if you choose her books together.

TALK ABOUT THE BOOK AND THE STORY

Sit quietly with your toddler and talk about the cover of the book, ask her about the shape of the book (square, rectangular or oblong) and when she is older, you can teach her about the author.

Ask her what she sees on the front page. Ask whether she can guess what the story is about. By talking to your toddler and asking her about the pictures in the book, you broaden her vocabulary and develop her language abilities. She could also guess what is going to happen in the story. This stimulates her reading skills.

SCHOOL-READINESS

If your child enjoys books and story time, she will be keen to learn to read much sooner. When she tries to read words herself, encourage her even if she makes mistakes. When you read to her, follow the words with your finger and allow her to 'read' too. A toddler who is guided in this way is usually ready to learn to read when she starts school, and that will help the teacher as well.

Learning to read is a basic skill we all need in our lives. The value of good reading skills simply cannot be emphasised enough. Your child will not only enjoy reading books, but will also enjoy using reference books later in her school career. She can learn so many other skills through books. This is how she learns about the wonders of the world. Books broaden her horizons so that she learns to look at her environment from different perspectives.

Memory

Memory is the ability to remember; to absorb new information, store it in the brain, and recall it later. Memory is essential for learning. Your child must remember previous experiences in order to learn to understand the world around her.

Short-term memory

Short-term memory is the part of the brain where information is ordered. Your child experiences the world around her through her senses. When she sees, hears, feels, tastes or smells, the information is held in the short-term memory for a few seconds. Information she considers important is then transferred to the long-term memory. Short-term memory is essential for language acquisition, following instructions, and interpreting the events of the day.

Long-term memory

Long-term memory is where information is stored. Your child can call up information in her long-term memory at any time and use it as she wishes. For example, she will not necessarily remember what she ate three days ago, but she would probably remember the finest details of her last birthday party. Long-term memory determines how children learn rhymes and songs, and how they relate events and stories of yesterday or the day before.

Attention span and concentration

The development of the memory is closely linked to attention span and concentration. Our attention span determines how long we can concentrate on one task. The ability to concentrate and pay attention to a specific task or situation is essential for remembering information.

An adult obviously has a longer attention span than a child. Your child's attention span and concentration increases tremendously between the ages of three and seven. She is gradually able to concentrate on specific tasks for longer periods and exclude other stimuli.

Games and activities that capture her imagination will help her to concentrate and her attention will not easily wander from what she is doing.

Games and activities for developing memory

Your child's attention span and memory will develop automatically as she grows, but there are specific activities that will stimulate this development. Remember, when you play games with her, that it is easier to remember actions than words. She will also remember something that really captures her imagination much better than something that does not interest her.

Babies and toddlers need **clues** and **repetition** to remember. Repeat the same stories and rhymes over and over, and play the same games with the same toys in the same place. Also store her favourite toys in the same place and follow the same routine – everything that is familiar to her serves as a clue to help her remember.

Use your infant's **name** at every opportunity, and repeat specific expressions in specific situations. Any familiarity will help her remember where she heard these words the previous time, and to associate specific words with specific situations.

Children find it easier to remember something you involve **more than one sense** at the same time, for example a toy that moves, but also makes sounds. Rhymes and songs with gestures and actions are great fun and most children just cannot get enough of them. This is one of the best activities for developing the memory.

Page through the same **books** with her at regular intervals, and keep the pages open for long enough to allow her to concentrate when she looks at the pictures. Ask her questions about the pictures.

Use ordinary playing cards for '**Snap**' and other games where recognition and grouping play a role.

Social and emotional development

Most parents' attention is directed mainly at the development of their children's physical and intellectual skills – the rate at which they grow and learn to sit, crawl, walk and talk – and do everything in their power to stimulate and promote these skills. The importance of social and emotional development is easily forgotten. However, social and emotional development can in fact be regarded as the foundation and purpose of every other kind of development, and as a parent, you can do much to ensure that your child is emotionally and socially well adjusted. The foundation for her social behaviour is laid at an early age. The way you interact with her, and the way she responds to you and her surroundings become part of her character.

Every baby has certain basic needs that must be met so that she can grow up as a normal and well-adjusted child:

- Safety and security
- Routine, discipline and consistency
- Love
- Uniqueness
- Acceptance, recognition and approval.

Safety and security

From birth, your baby is totally dependent on you to meet all her basic needs. If you love and cherish her, she will feel safe and secure.

If she feels safe and secure, she will have the courage to explore her surroundings. She will realise her urge to explore and want to learn more and more.

Routine, discipline, and consistency

A consistent routine for bath, feeding and sleeping times makes babies feel safe and secure – it makes the strange world they find themselves in more familiar, and is the first step in their emotional and social development. A daily routine at home remains very important for the development of your child. She must learn from an early age that she also has a responsibility at home and towards the people in her home.

Her home must be a safe haven, and this can only be so if there are clear rules and routine in the home. Children who are not subject to rules and routine at home will battle to adjust to the routine and discipline of a school environment.

Just as your child needs routine in order to feel safe and secure, she also needs discipline to be happy and well adjusted, because discipline also meets certain needs:

- She will know that there are limits of acceptable behaviour.
- She will know how she must behave if she wants to be praised for good behaviour – a sign of your acceptance and love.
- She will have the motivation to try to reach certain goals.
- She will learn self-control, which is the beginning of developing a conscience.
- She will be socially accepted, which will give her self-confidence and a feeling of security.

Be consistent with your discipline so that your child knows right from the beginning what is expected of her and what she can expect from you. The best way to teach your child about acceptable behaviour is to set an example for her to follow.

When it is necessary to discipline her, address her misdemeanour, not her as a human being. For example, say 'It was naughty to sit and break your crayons', not 'You are naughty'. Discipline should shape a child, not break her down. The punishment for misdemeanours should be fair and appropriate.

Taking away privileges as punishment works well with toddlers – they must learn to accept the consequences of their actions. Never punish your child in a fit of anger.

Love

Giving your child unconditional love, and forming a strong bond between you and her are the best foundation you can give her, not only for school-readiness, but also to be ready for life. Abundant natural physical contact, many hugs and kisses, and the assurance that you love her (tell her that you love her), will give her emotional security.

Fathers play an important role in the development of their children's emotional and social skills because they are an inseparable part of the environment of love and stability in which their children grow up. They should help at bath time, read stories, help with feeding, and play with their child as often as possible.

Uniqueness

Every child is unique and that uniqueness remains part of her – she wants to be allowed to be herself. She has a specific potential and you must help her to develop that potential in a relaxed and safe environment.

Do not make too many demands on her but, on the other hand, do not underestimate her either.

Give her space to develop her specific package of talents and aptitude, and to become a person in her own right.

Acceptance, recognition, and approval

Unconditional love and recognition of your child's uniqueness means that you should accept her – she must know that she is accepted as she is in order to build her self-confidence and to become a well-adjusted person.

Self-confidence is the most valuable gift any parent can give a child to take to school with her. She can only build self-confidence if she receives sincere, interested, and unselfish love at home. This will make her feel worthy and give her the courage to accept the challenges of life. Do not make acceptance and approval subject to how your child performs. Show her that you love and accept her, so that she knows she means a lot to you.

Praise your child regularly. She wants to please you and when you show that you notice and appreciate what she does, she will do it again – recognition is a very strong motivator.

Milestones in social and emotional development

From the beginning your baby's attention is directed at people – initially anybody who satisfies her basic needs and gives her attention.

By six months she begins to show clearly that she prefers the people closest to her, and she is afraid of strangers.

She likes other babies and children, and should have contact with other babies and children as much as possible.

By the age of one she will protest loudly when you leave her, because she does not know that you will come back. It will take a while before she realises and trusts that you will return.

She will gradually become possessive of her toys, and by the age of three she will know exactly what is hers and what is not. She will begin to identify with characters in stories.

She will believe that you know what is happening to her even when you are not there.

Birth to three months

Your baby is calmer with people she is familiar with, but will develop a closeness with whoever is caring for her. At this age, she stares intently at someone talking to her and moves her mouth.

By four to eight weeks she begins to smile and make gurgling sounds, and at three months she gurgles in response to your 'conversations' with her. She dislikes being deprived of social contact, and cries when left alone.

Four months

She takes an interest in people and recognises you and other people familiar to her. She shows her pleasure when she sees familiar people by waving her arms and kicking her legs, and shows that she is afraid of strangers by turning her face away and crying.

She gets bored when she is alone, and cries for attention. She laughs aloud when you play with her, stretching her arms out to be picked up.

Five to six months

She smiles at other babies and likes looking in the mirror, but does not realise that she is seeing her own reflection. Her response to an angry voice is different from her response to a friendly voice.

She smiles more readily at people she knows, and is more easily calmed by them when she is upset.

She does not form a tight bond with just anybody.

At six months it is part of her social behaviour to pull or stroke the hair of someone who is holding her, or to rub that person's nose.

Seven to nine months

She develops a fondness for specific people. She wants to be with you all the time (or with the person who takes care of her most of the time), and gets upset when you leave her.

She is afraid of strangers and strange places. She begins to socialise by imitating sounds and gestures.

She wants to please you, and stops an activity if you say 'no'. By ten months she becomes clingy and tightens her hold on you when strangers approach.

Twelve to 18 months

Your infant enjoys making you laugh, and pulls your clothing to get your attention. She responds to your moods and clearly shows when she is happy or frustrated.

She likes other children, but does not actually play with them and sometimes exhibits jealousy. At 18 months she begins to imitate people around her.

Two years

She begins to play with other children but does not know how to share her toys and can involuntarily hit and even bite other children – she enjoys the reaction it elicits. In fact, most of her behaviour is directed at getting attention. This age is a transition phase from baby to child, and your child will try to exert her will in all kinds of ways, for example by throwing tantrums (lying on the floor, kicking and screaming).

THREE YEARS

She is still very self-centred and sees most things from her own perspective. She enjoys talking about herself, her family and her possessions.

At this age, she can learn to wait until you have finished talking before she talks, but do not test her patience too much.

She responds to your emotions, and when you are unhappy or upset, she wants to comfort you and make you feel better.

She will offer to help you with small tasks – sorting the washing, setting the table, fetching the baby's nappy, and so on.

She becomes possessive about her toys and still expects to get everything she asks for, but throws fewer tantrums.

She shows empathy with characters in stories, and enjoys pretending to be someone else. She enjoys playing with certain friends and not with others, and misses her friends when she does not see them. Toddlers between three and six often have an imaginary friend.

She will be upset when her father leaves on a business trip, and needs reassurance that he will return, loves her, and will miss her.

FOUR YEARS

She can make a distinction between herself and other people, but still cannot really distinguish between her own feelings and thoughts, and those of other people. At this age she fantasises, and to her, fantasy and reality are still very close. Her behaviour is still very much directed at attracting attention. When she begins practising new activities, she likes new friends who participate in the same activities.

She becomes very competitive, and 'first' and 'best' become important to her. She begins to show social skills by greeting people, talking to them, and answering questions. If politeness is set as an example for her, she will say 'thank you' and 'please' and begin to show respect towards others in the home.

Five to six years

Friendships that your toddler form become more stable. At this age boys are more likely to befriend boys, and girls prefer girls, although individual friendships between boys and girls may still remain close. The approval of their friends is very important to them, and they will even try to win one another's favour by being naughty. Nevertheless, they are often bossy and find it difficult to play together and accept each other's suggestions.

Closer to the age of six your toddler begins to realise the value of compromise and negotiation. For example, she will suggest that her friend may play with her hula-hoop if she may ride on her friend's tricycle.

She doesn't mind sharing on condition she derives the biggest benefit from it. Competition between friends increases, not only during their activities but also about possessions. At this age, children often boast about what their parents own. However, their behaviour shows that they are aware of the approval or disapproval of people around them, and are generally more considerate than younger toddlers.

Your toddler cannot foresee the consequences of her actions and accept full responsibility for her possessions. She questions your authority, especially if she does not agree with you.

Games and activities for social development

Your child's toddler years are her most important formative years. The examples set by parents and others in the home are more important than prescribed rules of behaviour. Your child learns from you what is socially acceptable on the basis of your actions and behaviour.

Toddlers are very good imitators and will follow the example you set. Teach your toddler to be polite and considerate towards other people. Teach her to greet people and to say 'Please' and 'Thank you'.

Provide ample opportunities for your toddlers to play with friends. Children differ. One may have social needs as early as the age of three, others only at five. It also depends on the exposure to socialisation that they receive. Invite friends round to play with your child, or take her to play with friends. In the beginning you should be present during these visits.

Never leave your child with a friend if she does not want to stay there. This will cause anxiety and a loss of trust.

When friends come and play with your child, encourage them to play group games as well. Group games teach children that it is necessary to take turns, that there are basic rules that have to be followed, and that social interaction is fun.

Encourage your child, when you go to the park or beach, to talk to and play with other children. After all, you will be there to keep an eye on their interaction. At the beach you can join in and help to build sandcastles.

Healthy socialising

When your child starts school, she should be capable of healthy socialising. This requires three social skills: generosity, helpfulness and the ability to wait for her turn.

Teach your child to help others and to be friendly without being overly submissive and stifling the development of her own personality.

Teach your child to be sharing, not only with people in the home but also towards her friends. For example, teach her to share her toys with friends. Between the ages two to four, children find it difficult to share. For this reason you should explain carefully to your child that her friend will return the toy to her, and that she can play with it again later.

Share one sweet between her and her friend, for example, even if you have more, and explain that when they have eaten it, they can share another one. Also teach your child to respect other people's rights and possessions from an early age.

The realisation that people have to take turns is one of the most important social skills a child can learn. It is the basis of courtesy and thoughtfulness and is relevant at almost every level of life.

The secret is to help your child develop into a balanced person with sufficient self-confidence to insist on getting her turn without being dominating, or trying to dominate activities and conversations. The example that Mom and Dad set is very important in this respect.

Ready for school at an emotional level

Your child must not only be intellectually and physically ready for school – she must also be emotionally ready. This means she must be

- prepared to be separated from her parents;
- able to function independently (go to the toilet by herself and so on);
- able to hold her own in a group;
- able to postpone the satisfying of her emotional needs (for example, wait for her turn);
- able to show the necessary determination to complete a task;
- able to think independently when completing tasks;
- able to take responsibility.

Emotional intelligence

Emotional intelligence is the ability to interpret your own and others' feelings correctly and act on them in an appropriate way. Parents often believe that a high IQ is the most important requirement for success. However, research has shown that a high IQ is no guarantee for success in life.

Children who are in touch with their own emotions, who can 'read' other people's emotions, who can adjust their behaviour and attitudes to different circumstances, and who have self-confidence are more often successful.

Development of emotional skills

As a parent you can contribute to a large extent towards your child's development of emotional skills.

Problem-solving

Do not solve your child's problems for her. Instead, teach her how to solve her problems herself. The best way for her to learn is by the mistakes she is going to make. Teach her to think things through by asking questions such as 'What will happen if the cat changes into a lion?' 'What plan will you make if you don't have a house to live in?'

Teach her to make choices, not only about what she likes or wants to eat or wants to wear, but about the consequences of her choices. For example, ask 'What do you think will happen if you leave the door of the bird cage open?'

Talking about feelings

Teach your child to talk about her feelings. This is best done by setting an example. Express your feelings when you are angry or unhappy about something she did. Your child should learn from a young age that you also have feelings. In the same way, she should learn to express her feelings.

Talk to your child about emotions. Tell her that it is all right to feel afraid, angry or sad, and that she can also feel cheerful and happy. Help your child to experience a range of emotions, to acknowledge and recognise them, and to respond to them in an appropriate way. When she is angry with you, she may say so, but she may not hit you.

Acknowledge your child's emotions, but teach her that they may not serve as an excuse. For example, say 'I know you are hungry, but you may not have cookies before you

LAUGH AND THE WORLD LAUGHS WITH YOU

One of the most important gifts you can give your child is to teach her the pleasure of laughing. A sense of humour makes life so much easier – even when you are small! Research has shown that people are biologically programmed to smile. Most babies, including blind babies, begin to smile by four to eight weeks as an expression of pleasure. Babies who can see, smile more often as they grow older, while blind babies smile less often – in both cases in response to what they see (or don't see).

A baby who sees many smiling faces, will smile a lot. And a baby who smiles and beams happiness, receives as much and more in return. By the age of four months most babies laugh out loud – usually as part of human interaction – and what mother can resist that? A sense of humour develops along with your child's language skills. As her memory develops and she associates the right words with the right objects, she finds it screamingly funny when you give the wrong name for an object. A child of two will laugh in delight if you call her cat a teddy bear. You can expect your child between the ages of two to three to respond to jokes. Between the ages of three and four she will tell simple jokes herself, and most six and seven year olds can exhaust you with their endless jokes.

Don't allow your child to lose this natural urge – exploit it, encourage it, and teach her that the world laughs with you when you laugh.

have eaten your food'. If she throws a tantrum, wait until she has calmed down and ask her if there is something else she could have done instead of screaming. If your child regularly throws tantrums, give her a punching bag to use when she wants to express her anger. A cushion can serve this purpose.

Your child's emotional skills will be tested to an even greater extent among her friends.

Encourage her to talk to you about problems she may have with friends, and help her cope with these problems. For example, if a friend regularly bullies her, teach her to express her feelings and to say to the friend 'You hurt me and I don't like it. If you do it again, I won't play with you anymore'.

Teach her to deal with conflict in a polite manner, without hurting the other person's feelings.

As a family, discuss the feelings a family member may have experienced after some interaction with another person.

Talk about the reasons for people's actions and the effect these actions have on other people.

For example, say that the bully at school probably feels bad about himself and when he bullies others he feels better for a short while. This will make your child sensitive towards other people's feelings.

Emotions are genderless

Do not make a distinction between the emotions boys and girls experience. Boys experience emotions to the same extent as girls do.

Teach your child that boys may also be afraid and sad, not only girls, and that girls may get angry and insist on their rights, not only boys. Always bear in mind that you set an example that your child will follow.

If Dad shows that he is sad, a boy will accept it and know that he can also show how he is feeling.

Mutual respect

Teach your child from an early age not to think only of her own needs, but of those of others as well. When she pours a glass of cooldrink for herself, teach her to ask the others whether they want some too.

Teach her to respect other members of the family and to be considerate towards others, for example to leave the bathroom tidy for the next person who uses it.

Praise her when she shows such behaviour, for example 'You made me so happy because you hung up the towel so nicely'. This will reinforce positive behaviour.

Gratitude and humility

Teach your child to be greatful for what she has, and to have empathy with friends who may not enjoy the same privileges she does.

Encourage her to donate one of her toys to a welfare organisation, and tell her where the toy will be taken.

Teach her that every person is an individual, each with individual talents and skills. Teach her not to ridicule or laugh at friends who don't have the same skills as she does.

More tips

Parents who are loving towards each other and their child teach the child to show regard for others and form an emotional bond with their child. The way you apply discipline and the expectations you set for your child will determine her self-image to a great extent.

Acknowledge and emphasise her strong points, and give her sufficient recognition when she performs well. When she is naughty, make it clear that you disapprove of her behaviour, not of her. Never threaten her with withdrawal of your love, for example 'Mommy doesn't love you when you are so naughty'.

Your child's self-image is strongly influenced by the measure of success she achieves and experiences in her activities. Make sure that the demands you make on her and the activities you involve her in are not beyond her abilities. Note the following:

- Make time for your child, even if you are busy, and let her feel special.
- Teach her to be trusting.
- Teach her not to use swear words, even when her friends do.
- Teach her to say sorry when she has offended someone.
- Teach her to finish what she has begun, for example, not to stop doing gymnastics in the middle of a term.
- Teach her to communicate with adults. For example, let her order her own hamburger at a restaurant.

Characteristics of a toddler with high emotional intelligence

These characteristics also refer to a toddler of school-going age who is ready for school:

- She talks about her emotions.
- She empathises with others.
- She is optimistic and self-confident.
- She can solve her own problems (at a level appropriate to her age).
- She listens attentively.
- She can hold her own in a group of children of her own age.

8

Development of creativity

To be creative means to produce, think or do something original – it involves more than drawing pictures. The development of your child's creativity is an integral part of his total development. Every child is born with an innate urge to create, and this is as much a part of his humanness as it is to move and breathe. To be creatively active also contributes towards your child's emotional development.

Fantasy play and art (drawing and painting) are an emotional release for young children. For this reason they should be given every opportunity to express themselves creatively. It is part of their process of development. Through his play and drawing, your child expresses the things he learns and experiences. As soon as he can hold a pencil, he will start 'drawing' on any surface available. Initially the actual 'drawings' are of no importance – what is important is the fact that he is learning to hold a writing instrument. This is a skill he is going to need for the rest of his life. Even those toddlers who, at a later stage, seem disinclined to draw, should be encouraged to develop this skill.

Creative thinking

Although some people have a greater ability to think creatively than others, we all have this ability to some extent. Some may have more impressive talents than others, but being creative is part of all of us.

Everyone is able to produce something new in some way or another. Creativity and originality go hand in hand.

- New perspectives and possibilities are created that open up new worlds. For this reason, a child's ability to think creatively should be developed and stimulated. You can provide stimulation for your child in a purposeful way to encourage creativity.
- Your child can only develop creative thinking in a relaxed atmosphere. Maintain an appreciative, understanding and tolerant attitude about your child's attempts and efforts, as well as the mistakes he makes.
- A very creative child's behaviour can easily make him appear disobedient or wilful because he operates outside the normal patterns of behaviour. As a parent, you must exhibit sound judgement. Your child will learn by his mistakes and if you do not allow him to find his own way, you are denying him this opportunity. Regard his mistakes as steps towards creativity. Remember, he who does not dare does not win. Mistakes may often point to new beginnings.
- Never dampen your toddler's enthusiasm and excitement with negative criticism, and never dismiss his efforts as stupid, wrong or poor. Constant criticism dampens a child's spontaneity and his courage to think creatively. It blocks the development of creative thought and leads to a poor self-image. A child with a poor self-image can never really act creatively. On the other hand, positive feedback encourages him to experiment again and to use his imagination. It strengthens his self-image and gives him courage.
- Creativity is often restrained by parents who are too strict and authoritative. Your child should have the freedom to experiment and attempt and complete new things. Be tolerant and let him be, as long is he is not endangering himself or others.
- Fantasy play is important for the development of creative thought. This form of playing is the first expression of your child's imagination. It can begin as early as the age of two. After that it develops at an incredible pace and at four this kind of play can be exceptionally creative and contain several elements. Whether it is a group of little girls dressing up in their mothers' clothing and 'going out' or playing house, or a

couple of little boys working on a 'building site' in the sand with their buckets and spades and lorries and building material, it is an expression of imagination and fantasy. A child can make anything of ordinary objects – pebbles become cookies, the open area under the stairs a fairy tale castle, and the tree house a space ship. Never make fun of children engaged in fantasy play – rather play with them and encourage what they are doing.

Activities to develop creativity

Provide the right climate for playing. Allow your child to experiment and fantasise in his play. Let him act out the role he has chosen for himself.

- Give him thick wax crayons and paper, or an old book or magazine to draw or write in.
- Ask him about his works of art. Do not ask him 'What is that?', but rather 'Tell me about your picture'. If the lines he has drawn are 'Mommy', do not say 'But Mommy doesn't look like that' and then draw a stick figure for him to trace. This will smother his creativity. Rather encourage him to draw Daddy as well.
- When recognisable 'works of art' appear, for example a circle with two eyes which he identifies as 'Mommy', ask him 'Can Mommy also smell?' and point to your nose, and 'Can Mommy also eat?' and point to your mouth. This will teach him to observe details.
- Avoid giving him too many colouring in books. When your child measures his drawings against those in his books, he may not want to draw because he 'can't draw like that'.
- Read and tell your child stories again and again. Children never tire of hearing stories. Stories and fairy tales activate their imagination and will often appear in their fantasy play. They like to imagine themselves in the role of a character in a story or fairy tale. Read him poems as well. Sometimes, tell a story without an ending, and ask your child what he thinks is going to happen. Encourage him to tell you his own story.

- Ask your child to solve a hypothetical problem. Keep it simple at first, for example, 'What plan would you make if the house catches fire?' or 'How can we visit Grandpa if the car is broken?' Encourage him to draw what he thinks he would do.
- Listen to music with your child. Ask him to execute the movements he hears in the music with his body. Ask him what the music makes him think about, and how it makes him feel. Walk in the veld with him and let him listen to the singing of the birds. Teach him what sounds the different birds make. Show him pretty wildflowers, autumn leaves or patterned bark while you walk. If he wants to, ask him to draw what he saw when you arrive home.
- Don't throw away cardboard boxes. Give them to your toddler and see where his imagination leads him. Help him glue together boxes of different sizes and to paint them, so that they represent whatever he wants them to.

Milestones in the development of drawing skills

All children's drawing skills follow the same stages of development, but not necessarily at exactly the same age. It depends on their physical development, as well as their world of experience. The general milestones remain more or less the same.

Most infants begin to pick up crayons at the age of 18 months and make marks on paper, the floor, walls or cupboards. This first scribbling means nothing more to him than that he has made something happen – he moves the crayon over the paper (wall, floor or cupboard) and leaves marks behind. Over the next couple of years he will begin to draw what he sees around him, and his drawings will give you insight in the way he sees his surroundings.

EIGHTEEN MONTHS

Your infant's uncontrolled scribbles do not represent anything. He handles play dough purely for pleasure and does not try to create anything with it.

TWO YEARS

Your toddler begins to discover the connection between the movements he made and the marks on the paper, and he will consciously repeat the same movement. This is called controlled scribbling. All children use more or less the same scribbles, and all possible shapes are inherent in the scribbles, which are necessary for his drawing and writing skills at a later stage. He rolls play dough but still does not make anything specific.

THREE TO FOUR YEARS

Your toddler tells you what his scribbles represent, although you cannot see the likeness between what he drew and what he says he drew. Use of colour is unrealistic and he often prefers only one colour. He can paint with a thick brush. Drawings contain circles, crosses, squares and dots combined in different ways. He rolls out play dough and uses biscuit cutters, but remains more fascinated by the play dough than with what he can do with it.

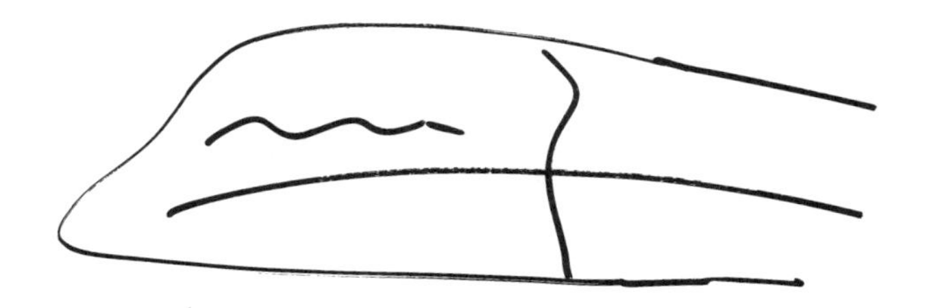

FOUR TO FIVE YEARS

Now your toddler is deliberately trying to combine circles and lines, and his scribbles more or less correspond with the object he is drawing. The first recognisable shapes are usually that of people.

The first person is usually a head with legs. His eyes are drawn prominently because eye contact is so important to toddlers. Gradually other things become important to him as well. For example, if his father holds his hand when they cross a road, he will draw the hand as well.

He will also begin to draw animals and houses. At this age the representation of people, animals and houses changes constantly. The people and objects your toddler draws look as if they are floating in the air, because spatial expression is still absent. He also often places himself in the middle of the drawing because at this age he is still very much at the centre of the world.

Use of colour is still unrealistic and does not correspond with nature. He will draw purple people and blue trees.

He makes balls and sausages with play dough and puts them together to represent people and animals.

Six to seven years

Your toddler draws all people the same. He draws the same basic human figure to represent the whole family, but draws the figures in different sizes and indicates gender with hair and clothes.

He enlarges things that are important to him in his drawings, and leaves unimportant things out. If he has earache, he is likely to draw the sore ear large and the other one small.

He will include everything he believes should be there. His idea of a house in most cases has a chimney drawn at a slant on the roof, even if there is an electric stove and no fireplace in the house. The door is low because he can walk through it, and the windows high because he cannot open them himself.

He draws animals he knows with faces like those of people. He draws objects on a base line (the grass) and a tree that is higher than the house, and the flowers smaller.

He also draws transparent pictures, for example kittens in his cat's stomach, or a stick figure with clothing over the lines and features of the body.

Movement is also represented graphically, for example an animal's feet will be wide apart if it is running. He likes to draw the sun rising or birds flying.

His use of colour becomes more realistic: a tree has a brown trunk and green leaves.

Materials for activities

You can keep your toddler creatively occupied for hours on end and it needn't cost you an arm and a leg. These are the basics:

- Thick paint/finger paint (*see* page 119);
- Thick brushes (one for each colour paint);
- Other applicators such as a small sponge, crumpled plastic bag or plastic wrap, carved shapes and so on;
- Plastic egg containers (for paint in different colours);
- Wax crayons;
- Paper (large sheets) and easel;
- Play dough (*see* page 20 and below) and biscuit cutters
- Salt ceramic dough (*see* below)

Salt ceramic dough

1 cup salt
1/2 cup corn flour
3/4 cup water

Mix together everything in a saucepan and stir over medium heat until the mixture thickens and forms a 'ball'. Remove from heat and place dough on foil.

Allow to cool slightly and knead thoroughly. Place in airtight container if not used immediately. Knead again before use to soften.

Any objects your child makes with this dough can be placed in the sun to dry (it usually hardens within 3-5 days). It can also be baked in an oven (low heat) for 2 hours.

Both watercolour and poster paint are suitable for painting the dried objects.

Play dough for one

1 cup flour
1/2 cup salt
2 t cream of tartar
1 cup water
1 T oil
1 t food colouring

Sift flour, salt and cream of tartar. Mix liquid and colouring in a saucepan over medium heat. Stir in all the dry ingredients. Stir continuously until mixture forms a ball (watch it, as it burns easily). Remove from stove, leave until cool enough to handle and knead thoroughly. Store in airtight container until you want to use it.

FONDANT

1/3 cup margarine
1/3 cup syrup
1/2 t salt
1 t vanilla
food colouring
500 g icing sugar

Mix all ingredients except icing sugar over a low heat in a saucepan until melted (do not let it boil). Leave to cool and add the sifted icing sugar. Mix and knead thoroughly until smooth (add more icing sugar if necessary for non-stick 'play dough'). Let your child make objects of this dough to his heart's content. It feels like clay and can be eaten when everyone has finished playing.

Baking cake

Let your child and his friends each make their own cup cake dough when you bake a cake. Bake it for them and let them decorate it themselves. Boys will enjoy this as much as girls.

CUP CAKE DOUGH FOR ONE

2 t margarine
2 t sugar
2 T egg mixture (1 egg, 1 cup milk, 1 t vanilla, beaten)
3 t self-raising flour
pinch of salt

Let each child make the dough in a plastic bowl that he can handle. Cream margarine and sugar together. Add egg mixture and mix slightly. Add self-raising flour and salt and mix until smooth. Spoon into paper cup, place in muffin pan and bake until golden brown (at 180 °C/350 °F).

Give each child some icing sugar and a variety of coloured sweets to decorate his own cup cake.

Fun with paint

Spatter paint: Make up some powder paint and give your toddler a large brush and a large sheet of paper on some old newspapers. Spatter paint with a tooth brush on a smaller scale is also great fun.

Finger paint is not necessarily only meant for fingers and hands. Allow your toddler to create unique works of art by using his feet – the paint is easily cleaned off.

FINGER PAINT

Mix two heaped tablespoons of starch powder (corn flour) with a little water until creamy. Add boiling water while stirring continuously until you have a thick runny paste (like thick custard).

Pour into containers, add powder paint to get the desired colour, cool and put the lids on.

Put a small amount of each colour in small paint containers or bottles for your toddler to use.

Small amounts of paint can also be poured into a muffin pan to be used for finger paint projects.

Mix yellow and blue for green; red and yellow for orange; red and blue for purple.

The role of the pre-primary school

No school can substitute the role that you as a parent play in your child's development during the first five years. Pre-primary school has its own specific role in preparing your child for 'real school'. This preparation consists of:

- Supporting and aiding your toddler's development during the first five years before she enters her formal school career.
- Identifying, by means of evaluation during the daily programme, where your child may still be lagging behind.
- Providing opportunities to address possible problems in the pre-primary classroom situation.
- Identifying learning problems, and referring toddlers at an early stage for further evaluation and/or occupational therapy.
- Ensuring that your toddler's development meets the norm for her age group in all areas – physical, intellectual, emotional and social.

Although pre-primary schools prepare toddlers for formal learning, no school can make a child ready for school sooner that she would otherwise have been.

No toddler can be forced to maturity. Each one develops at her own pace. Your child is unique – accept her as such. Unnecessary pressure simply leads to all kinds of problems. A toddler who can read and write and do maths before entering school is not necessarily ready for formal teaching – she may be emotionally and socially completely immature, in which case she will have more trouble adapting than a child who does not yet have any maths or writing skills.

How do you choose a pre-primary school?

All parents want the very best for their children and the best pre-primary school is a good start. The first pre-primary school or play group your child attends will play an important role in her attitude towards school for the foreseeable future, and possibly for the rest of her school career. If for practical or financial reasons you are not limited to a specific school, obtain as much information as possible about pre-primary schools in your area and do your homework before making a choice.

Pre-primary school is intended for children between the ages of five and six years. This is the preparation year for formal teaching. Most pre-primary schools accept children from the age of four, but then they have a less formal

programme for a year. In terms of current legislation, your child may go to 'proper school' only during the year she turns seven.

Religious or educational approach

First decide what matters most to you in your choice of a pre-primary school. For example, if you want your child's education to have a specific religious or educational approach, your choice will be smaller than if you are simply looking for a 'good' school. Visit the schools you are considering, and make your choice according to your child's needs.

A balanced programme

Pre-primary education should address your child's entire development and ensure that she develops her full potential. A good pre-primary school's educational programme will be child-centred. It will stimulate your child's social, emotional, motor, perceptual, mental and physical development. The activities will include the following: discussions, music, movement circles, creative art activities, time to play with educational toys and puzzles, free outdoor play, among others with sand and water, on climbing apparatus, and so on.

Everything at the school will be aimed at providing a stimulating and enriching learning environment, where all facets of a child's development receive attention. Children are therefore equipped with skills not only for school-readiness, but which will enable them to take their place as well-balanced adults in society. A good self-concept is therefore crucial.

The programme and approach must make provision for the fact that all children do not progress at the same pace, so that each child is able to participate according to her ability, and still learn to function in a group context.

Practical arrangements

Ask the school for a copy of their prospectus. This should contain all the most important information about the school. That will help you to decide whether the school's policy and approach correspond with what you feel is important in your child's education. If you have a prospectus you can always refer to it if you think the school is departing from its stated policy. And if you do not agree with the school's policy, rather look for another school immediately.

- School fees should be used efficiently, and the school should be able to submit financial statements.
- Enquire about disciplinary measures. If toddlers are smacked, bullied or humiliated in front of their friends, give that school a wide berth and look for another school.
- Establish what the numbers are. A ratio of twenty toddlers per teacher is realistic. Many schools use assistant teachers when this ratio is higher than 30 to one. This means that your toddler will always be in the care of an adult while the teacher is occupied with another group of toddlers, or has to deal with some crisis or another.
- Make sure the staff have suitable formal teaching qualifications. Already at the pre-primary stage, teaching is not only about what your child learns, but about how she is taught. Your task as a parent during the first five years of her life is to teach her that it is fun to learn. This task must be continued by the pre-primary school.

Appearance of school and equipment

When choosing a pre-primary school for your toddler, you may, in contrast with the proverb, judge the book by its cover. Clean and well-tended grounds and buildings, neatly painted toys and climbing apparatus, hygienic bathrooms and toilets are the external signs of staff who care. The opposite is also true. Besides, broken and dirty apparatus and facilities hold safety and health risks. So do have a close look at the condition of the buildings, equipment, and so on before making your final decision.

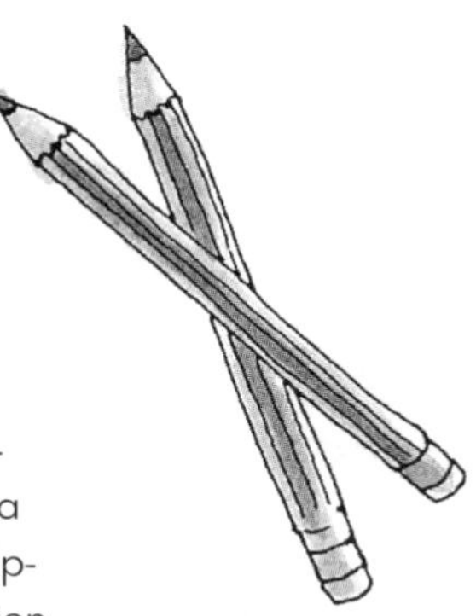

Professionalism of teachers

In all schools, the quality of the education a child will receive depends on the professionalism of its teachers.

A professional teacher will remain updated on changes in the education system. She will constantly evaluate her equipment and programme to ensure that it meets the requirements of each child as an individual, and that these work in a group context as well. If changes are necessary, a good pre-primary school should be financially and professionally capable of implementing the changes.

Evaluation

Establish how children's progress is evaluated, and whether records are kept of their progress. Regular formal evaluation is essential to identify possible problems at an early stage and to address these.

Children's level of school-readiness must also be regularly tested, so that specific areas, which may require additional attention, are identified and the necessary steps taken.

Pre-primary teachers play an important role in the timely identification of learning or physical problems, for example hearing or visual disability. Establish what procedures are followed when a possible problem is identified. Schools should have an open policy in this regard that includes parents.

Interaction with parents

Find out what the school's policy is concerning parents visiting the school. Parents should know that they will be welcome at the school at all times, and that they will have access to their child and her environment without interrupting the class programme.

Rather stay away from a school that does everything behind closed doors and where parents are not welcome during school hours. There should be a warm, relaxed atmosphere at the school in which your child can feel at home and happy.

Ask beforehand to be allowed to sit and observe during a school day so that you can establish whether toddlers are actively engaged in the learning process.

A good teacher will encourage learning by planning interesting and exciting activities and by creating a safe environment in which children can develop their skills. With the necessary self-confidence and a positive self-image, any toddler should be able to overcome most stumbling blocks.

Parent involvement at your child's school is crucial. Your child's progress at school is not only the responsibility of the teacher, but yours as well. You must support your child and show an interest in what she is learning, as well as how she is learning.

You should also be on the look-out for signs of unhappiness or tension in your toddler. Speak to the teacher if you are worried about something. Remember, you are working towards the same goal.

Practical hints

Talk to parents with children at the particular school. You will quickly find out whether the school meets their expectations. The degree of their satisfaction will therefore serve as a measure for you. If you know of parents who have moved their children to another school, ask them why they made this decision. There may be a practical reason, but there may also be an underlying problem you should know about.

A school is judged by its people. Toddlers will soon enough show that something is amiss. Watch how they interact with one another. Are they taught to respect one another? What kind of interaction takes place between staff members and between them and the toddlers? Keep in mind that your child's pre-primary teacher is his role model.

In conclusion

Not all of us are in a position to choose a pre-primary school for our children. Sometimes they have to go to a particular school for practical or financial reasons. Whatever the circumstances, become actively involved in your child's school. Become part of the school community by engaging in activities arranged by the school, or declare yourself willing to serve in a committee, the parent-teacher society, or the control board. Parent involvement is the best guarantee that the education your child receives is what you want for her.

Is my child ready for school?

When children start school for the first time, unique demands are made on them. For example, they will have to:

- Get used to being away from their family and home;
- Communicate with and relate to strangers;
- Hold their own in a group (often large) and be able to assert themselves;
- Be capable of handling conflict and criticism;
- Be capable of switching from spontaneous and informal play to a more formal way of learning and working;
- Be able to work without being constantly praised;
- Be able to work on their own;
- Be capable of working quietly and calmly;
- Be capable of expressing their needs in words;
- Be capable of using basic language and writing skills in order to learn to read, write and draw;
- Be capable of concentrating and completing tasks.

What is required of your child?

This section is a brief summary of the broader discussions in the rest of the book. Although the official age for entering school is currently seven years and because children are usually formally tested for school-readiness at their pre-primary school, you can use the following information as a guideline to determine whether your child is ready for this important milestone in her life.

School-readiness implies that your child is ready to tackle her school career **with a reasonable measure of success**, and she should be able to meet the requirements discussed next.

- Your child should see and hear well. Take her to a paediatrician for a thorough examination. He or she will be able to confirm that your child does not have any problems.
- Your child must be physically well developed. She must be capable of touching her right ear with her left hand stretched over her head.
- She must be able to function independently and do things for herself; for example going to the toilet, dressing, bathing, and fastening her shoes.
- She should have a good body image – know that she has two feet, one nose, ten fingers, and so on. She must be able to name and touch the different body parts, and touch one part with another, for example touch her foot with her elbow.
- She must know that she has a left side and a right side, and not confuse right with left. She should have a dominant hand, foot and eye.
- She should have a good grasp of time, know the days of the week, and understand and use the concepts morning, afternoon and evening, today and tomorrow correctly.
- Her self-confidence should be reasonably well developed so that she can assert herself and not be bullied.
- Her language should be sufficiently developed and she should have a reasonable vocabulary. She should be capable of expressing herself in language and also understand an instruction given to her. She should be able to carry out two instructions correctly when given together.
- She should be able to concentrate well and function in the context of a group. In other words, she should be able to sit quietly, listen and be attentive.
- She should be able to copy figures, letters and simple objects.

Characteristics of typical toddlers

Read this section together with the milestones shown at the various areas of development.

Well-adjusted three-year-olds

Three-year-old toddlers have more self-confidence than two-year-old toddlers, and are proud of their abilities. They often reject the help of adults because they are determined to do things themselves. Their toys belong only to them and they protect them. They also derive a lot of pleasure from their toys. At this age they do not like to share. Daily events in their lives are a great adventure to them and they express this enjoyment in their play. Their observation of things in their surroundings sharpens and they are able to notice details. They are very interested in their immediate surroundings and ask endless questions. Often questions are asked merely to get attention. They enjoy finger games and stories in which there is a lot of repetition. They are also fond of making constant comments when a story is told or read to them.

At this age, toddlers have fixed ideas about certain things and often become very angry when they do not have their own way. Socially they are not ready to become involved in a group and communication with other three-year-olds is still very limited. Their emotional development has not progressed much yet, and at this age they can develop all kinds of fears. In spite of their budding independence, toddlers still have a great need for love and physical contact.

Well-adjusted four-year-olds

At this age toddlers enjoy discovering and experimenting, and they are interested in nature and natural phenomena. They are very active and find it difficult to sit still for long. They move and run without effort. They play with friends of both sexes, but always have a special friend who is important to them. Four-year-old toddlers fight and enjoy telling tales when they play, but are learning to assert themselves.

Four-year-olds have discovered that certain words evoke reactions from adults and will use them constantly. The scope of their interest broadens; it extends beyond their immediate surroundings and they constantly ask questions. Fairy tales and stories that satisfy their curiosity, for example how a tractor, fire engine, helicopter or the police work, are popular with this age group.

Their imagination is still as strong as when they were three. They still act impulsively, often become restless, and are easily excited. They also become aggressive when thwarted. Their sense of humour has developed further and they like to identify with characters in funny stories.

WELL-ADJUSTED FIVE-YEAR-OLDS

At this age, many toddlers attend pre-primary school, which clearly plays a role in their social adjustment and skills. A five-year-old toddler has a will of her own and is fairly independent of other people. They enjoy playing with children of their own age and blossom as social beings. They are very sensitive to social situations and are very aware of their status as a person. They are ashamed when they do not meet the expectations of others. They are able to improve their behaviour when necessary. They are also loyal to their teachers and friends. At this age, they can easily feel rejected and suddenly refuse to go to school. They make excuses because they are afraid of rejection or that they will not meet expectations. This problem must be handled carefully, since a toddler may feel unwanted at home if she is forced to go to school. At school she may be afraid that she cannot cope.

Most five-year-olds are self-assured and have excellent control over their motor skills. They begin to show an interest in children from other countries and the things they do. Bible stories can successfully be told to children in this age group. They are also mature enough to understand basic natural phenomena. Five-year-old toddlers have a more subtle sense of humour than four-year-old toddlers. They understand difficult words and can think logically. They enjoy a variety of stories that can now be longer and more complex.

WELL-ADJUSTED SIX-YEAR-OLDS

Toddlers at this age are very lively and investigate everything under the sun. They like to feel important and are inclined to praise themselves. They are very self-centred and like to compete with their friends. They are often impulsive and very spontaneous. Positive motivation is very important at this stage. Boys, in particular, often clown around.

Six-year-old toddlers are hungry for learning. They are very observant, ask many questions, form ideas and come to their own conclusions. They become impatient when they do not achieve immediate success with any task. When they battle and cannot do things to their own satisfaction, they quickly become frustrated and even protest loudly. Their opinions change frequently and they are inclined to boast. Their moods are also erratic. One minute they may be full of life and then suddenly become withdrawn and dejected. They are energetic and sometimes destructive, especially if they are not kept busy and stimulated. They can also become engrossed in their own activities. They enjoy group play and like doing things with their hands. They like dismantling things to see how they work. They have a rich imagination which they give free rein to, and they enjoy telling stories. Adventure stories and those about people from foreign countries are their favourites. There must be enough action and the problems must be solved. They also like stories that contain unknown elements, and stories that describe people's feelings. Some toddlers begin to read at this age and will practise this with enthusiasm.

WELL-ADJUSTED SEVEN-YEAR-OLDS

Children are much calmer and self-assured at this age, and are usually good listeners. They are also at times careless, complaining, whining, sad and shy. They ponder about things. It is characteristic of children at this age that they take more out of a relationship than they put into it.

At seven, toddlers are more aware of themselves as people in their own right, and are considerate towards others. They hero-worship their fathers and are often very attached to their teachers. They are eager to help when the mood strikes them, and can distinguish between acceptable and bad behaviour. Their use of language is good and they have a good grasp of time, seasons, months of the year, days of the week, and so on. Some seven-year-olds can read well and enjoy it too. Children of this age love humorous stories. Stories for this age can be longer than those for six-year-olds, with lots of action and events in rapid succession.

On the way to self-sufficiency

Toddlers increasingly long for independence and grab every opportunity to do things for themselves. Independence gives children self-confidence and self-respect. To them, it is so much better to say 'I can' than 'I can't'. Toddlers must learn not only to dress themselves, to eat and use the toilet by themselves – they must also learn to do it without being told. A child who cannot get up in the morning and dress herself without being told to do so, is still dependent on you.

Milestones to independence

Independence not only strengthens your child's self-image, it also makes her life away from you so much easier. Keep the guidelines on the following pages in mind, and help her to become a self-sufficient person. Anticipate that she 'can', but help her surreptitiously when you see that she cannot manage something by herself. Do not help her immediately when she struggles with something – wait until she asks. Then help her to do it 'herself', rather than doing it 'for her'. Praise her each time she manages to do something on her own.

One year

Your child can sleep by herself, and keeps playing when you leave the room for a while. She can eat finger food by herself, and drink from a cup with a spout.

Two years

Two-year-olds can wipe their faces with a facecloth and try to brush their teeth (even if you have to do it again). They insist on eating by themselves, but it is very messy (self-sufficiency should never be discouraged just because of the mess). They learn to use the potty. They try to dress themselves but can only just handle clothing without buttons or other fasteners. They can play by themselves for short periods.

Three years

They no longer need nappies during the day and ask to go to the toilet (you have to help). They can dress themselves, but still cannot fasten buttons and zippers. Eating is less messy, but they

still cannot butter their bread. They can put away their toys and keep themselves busy in the house or garden. The want to brush their own teeth and wash themselves.

FOUR YEARS

They can dress and undress themselves, and unfasten largish buttons in front and on the side. They can fasten buttons in front and wash and dry their own hands. They brush their teeth by themselves. Going to the toilet is something they can do, although you still have to help them with the wiping part. When you remind them, they can blow their nose, and put their hand in front of their mouth when they cough or sneeze. Pouring drinks for themselves is fun, and they are able to stay dry during the night. Small tasks, like helping to put the washing away, can be done without supervision.

FIVE YEARS

They can distinguish between the front and back of their clothing. They dress themselves, but sometimes still need help with fastening their clothes. They can wash their face and hands, and dry them. They can help themselves to a piece of bread, an apple, or cooldrink when they are hungry or thirsty, and are can handle their toilet routine without help.

SIX YEARS

They can wash their face and wipe their nose, and bath without supervision. They can handle a knife and spread their bread with soft butter. They can lace up their shoes and tie a knot. At this age, children like to organise their own games and complete tasks without waiting for someone to tell them how to proceed, or needing praise for what they have managed. They can manage without you for longer periods, and go to play with friends without your having to accompany them.

Conclusion

Remember, even if your child has all the necessary physical skills in all the areas of development, but still does not have the inner skills such as independence, perseverance, resilience, the ability to concentrate on a set task, endurance, self-discipline and daring, she is like a brand-new car without an engine.

Bibliography

Einon, Dorothy 1999: *Learning Early*, Marshall Publishing, London

Landsdown, Richard & Walker, Marjorie 1991: *Your Child's Development: from birth to adolescence*, Frances Lincoln, London

Pieterse, Martie 1999: *Clever Talk*, Metz Press, Bellville

Stoppard, Miriam 1993: *New Baby Care Book*, Struik, Cape Town

Umansky, Kaye & Fisher Chris 2001: *Nonsense Animal Rhymes*, Oxford University Press, Goodwood